Tour of Insanity: Manifesto for Better Home Design

REMODELED

Kelly Mitchell & Matt Zakutny

AuthorHouse™
1663 Liberty Drive
Bloomington, IN 47403
www.authorhouse.com
Phone: 833-262-8899

This book is printed on acid-free paper.

ISBN: 978-1-6655-4525-9 (sc)
ISBN: 978-1-6655-4524-2 (e)

Library of Congress Control Number: 2021923754

Print information available on the last page.

Published by AuthorHouse 11/26/2021

CONTENTS

INTRODUCTION

For the most part, urban planning is the masterful execution of precise grids knitting together homes and community features with access to utilities. Structured, well-thought plans allow neighborhoods to capitalize on the goods and services of their community. You would think the same amount of care in planning would be present in the form and function of home design and architecture. Urban planning, architecture, and design should include a wiggle room strategy in the planning phase to adapt to a changing world. Unfortunately, the wiggle has not been adopted.

Insanity is doing the same thing over and over and expecting different results. People, we are certifiable when it comes to the aesthetics and architecture of home design. To add insult to injury, our homes are getting smarter. It started with the little personal secretary perched on the counter; her name is Alexa. We scream at Alexa to fetch us this or that or even argue with her when we are bored (yes, I know you've done it).

Today, we have smart appliances that speak to each other without human intervention. For example, the thermostat will keep track of when you are home and report ways to conserve energy, saving you heaps of money. The sprinkler system alerts you to leaks and identifies where they are located. The refrigerator teams up with a mobile app to make your grocery list; Jetsons eat your heart out.

With advancements in technology, we continue to do same shit different day with the components in and outside our home. This book is intended to be a tour through the insanity we glide through every day. Most days without thinking about it. Not thinking about it is the problem.

I know you have scanned through a room in your home and fixated on something. Then, after successfully remembering why you entered the space in the first place, you think - *Why Is This Here? What Function Can This Possibly Serve?* This manifesto answers those questions. This tour provides solutions to inspire and instigate change in an area that seems to be explained by - *It's just always been that way.*

If you are looking for direct, quick-fix solutions or guidance in a Bob Villa kind of way, this book is not for you; walk away. Instead, we highlight interesting facts of *why* things are the way they are and couple the *why* with possible solutions. The practical information provided encourages you to renovate your home. As a bonus, this book also serves as a kindling for fiery, intriguing conversations at dinner parties, vetting the right dating partner, or a coffee table book to break the awkward silences when in-laws are visiting.

We say it's time for a revolution to no longer blindly accept old ways and embrace new ideas in the spirit of entertainment and innovation. Stop tolerating the non-functional 'annoyance' factor in home planning and design. Instead, participate in a way to stop the insanity. Let's take a tour, shall we?

CHAPTER 1

Carpeted Bathrooms: But Why The Rugs, Though?

The average person spends 92 <u>days</u> of their life on the porcelain throne. That amount *does not* include time spent primping ourselves for work, date night, or seeking sanctuary from family at Thanksgiving dinner.

Bathrooms are a highly-coveted space. You don't honestly know who someone is until they are confined in a home with five people and one bathroom; it's emotional. With the paramount importance of quality time that we spend in the bathroom: *Why is the bathroom not better matched to our needs?*

Who Started The Insanity?

The concept of detouring waste away from the home goes back 5,000 years with urban planning in the Indus Valley, Rome, Egypt, and several other ancient civilizations. However, the actual swirling bowl came much later in the 1500s from the godson of Queen Elizabeth I and the elbow grease of the Industrial Revolution. Back in the day, it was commonplace for 20 people to handle business between flushes (Ewww!).

But when did the actual bath*room* come into play? The room that secludes our bath and bidet activities? The room shrouding our releases and allowing privacy to ponder our thoughts in peace? More importantly, who started the TILE floors? Isn't it always the bloody Romans?

Bathing publicly before entering a sacred space or socializing in large thermal baths was practiced in many places of the world. However, the wealthy Romans separated public and private baths, elevating the bathroom to another level. Although Romans would still ritually bathe in public, they incorporated a personal space in their home, distinguishing private and public hygiene and relaxation habits.

Romans who could afford it would build a separate room containing a private, heated bath and equip it with ointment, incense, combs, mirrors, and even a working toilet system. Romans were skilled architects; mastery level. Their innovations were unmatched for centuries and still lurk in structures and urban planning strategies today. Their elite planning and foresight are why every bathroom mimics Roman design.

Romans are credited with molding cement, creating celebrated masterpieces in museums, and lingering on university and library grounds. Romans designed the majestic archways viewed across the globe. And, Romans lent their skills in manipulating cement to the lowly bathroom floor tiles. AH-HAH, our tile villain!

Privatizing Bathrooms: Sharing Is Not Caring

Before the 19th century, the cause of diseases were believed to be spontaneously combusted chaos or hexed on you because of sinful acts you participated in. Doctors and commoners firmly believed that if you were acutely ill, demons possessed you. It was a bit intense. Luckily, we began exploring new theories of how germs are spread that were far less likely than demons. Fortunately, we put rhyme to reason and discovered lack of basic hygiene *was* the demon.

This discovery was a turning point in medical history. The epiphany led to hospital facilities and sophisticated treatments. Well, more sophisticated than demons or spontaneous combustion anyway. Vaccines were developed, and the miracle drug, penicillin, ensured our survival. The 19th century was plagued by demon germs (literally) but science helped us vanquish the epidemics of:

- Cholera
- Smallpox
- Typhus
- Yellow fever
- Plague; and
- Scarlet fever

Thanks to disease transmission studies, cleanliness (with soap), and improved hygiene practices, private bathrooms were all the rage. As a result, private bathrooms became a prominent staple in every household (not just the wealthy ones), promoting wellness and sanitary conditions.

The industrial revolution provided hot and cold running water, flushable toilets, and full-size luxurious bathtubs, sinks, and showers. A wave of gas heaters and plumbed houses erupted all over the country. In 1889, the electric water heater was introduced, blowing the minds of every citizen.

Homes now included a private family restroom with intricate tiled patterns and spruced-up accessories replacing the old wooden elements (#trending). A new world opened up and formed the foundation for the bathrooms we know today, sort of.

The Age Of Carpeted Bathrooms

When you utter the words 'carpet' and 'bathroom' in the same sentence, people's buttholes pucker. Shortly after the involuntary body shiver, their answer slaps you in the face - **NO!** There are some *extreme* opinions about carpets in bathrooms. So, how did carpets in bathrooms start, and how did it earn this reaction?

For the most part, <u>bathrooms</u> through the 1950s looked identical to today's restrooms, except for the lime green color. *Sanitary* was the primary focus and aesthetics were secondary. Then something happened, the big bang in bathrooms. When Romans aren't to blame, it's usually hippies.

During the 1960s and 70s, shag carpeting - or carpeting of any kind - was seen as a luxury item. That luxury item crawled across the bathroom floor wall to wall. The 70s were full of opposition:

- Opposition to war
- The opposition of submissive women
- The opposition of government institutions; and mostly
- Opposition to *tiled floors* in bathrooms

For examples see: (<u>https://www.sunset.com/</u>)

An ocean of shag carpeting showed its brazen personality (mostly in green or orange) across bathrooms in America. Americans reveled in its unsurpassed urine, dirt and mold trapping technology. If you lost an earring, it was gone forever, lost in the dense fabric that is shag. In all fairness, the carpeted bathroom revolution *really* started in the 1950 post-war era when women could afford the luxuries previously cut off due to shortages. One of those luxuries was carpet. But, it was the <u>70s</u> era that celebrated the thick carpet that was both on the floor *and* stretched over the toilet - delivering the complete shock & awe factor. If you were exceptionally skilled and fashion adept, you had *rugs* laying on top of the carpets. One <u>Reddit</u> user reminisces:

"My parents' house came with a carpeted half bath. And laundry/utility room, kitchen, and dining room. This meant that the door to the backyard had carpet next to it. Even better, it wasn't regular carpet, it was 'outdoor' carpet where the pad is attached and the whole shebang is glued to the floor. The 70s was a dark time for some people. I imagine drugs were involved. Don't carpet your bathroom."

The age of overconsuming carpet was short-lived. By the early 1980s, tile had returned to the bathroom. We could say the drug-induced haze had cleared as to why tile reappeared in bathrooms. However, it is more likely that carpets in bathrooms ended because of mold and the high maintenance involved in keeping a carpeted bathroom clean. When the Center for <u>Disease</u> Control & Prevention (CDC) steps in and says, *Stop carpeting your bathrooms. It's a health hazard* - people generally take notice. For those that still needed convincing, Bob <u>Villa</u>, the grandmaster of home decor, displayed this on his website:

"Carpet is a magnet for moisture and its by-products. Between steamy vapor from the shower and water dripping off your body, bathroom carpet is bound to get wet—and soak up the moisture like a sponge."

A word of caution, don't Google 'moisture by-product', lesson learned. Out with the old and in with the new. There are some things about the 70s that I miss. Like those monster space heaters with red hot coils spaced far enough to get a child's finger through the protection grate. Those were the days. My grandma constantly plugged one in near the water, on shag carpet to keep the room toasty for my bath. I also basked in the glowing orange hue from the warming light on the ceiling. I didn't realize until I was older that I had grown up in a cult horror film. It explains a lot. Anyway, here we are, back where we started, taking our chances with tile flooring.

Bathroom Tile Evolutions

Did you know approximately 235,000 people over age 15 visit emergency rooms every year because of injuries sustained in the bathroom? But, more importantly, are you aware of how unsettling it is to step *barefoot* on an ice-cold floor and be stunned for a few seconds with the searing uncomfortableness of it all?

To plenty of people, 'roughing it' is stepping out of a hot shower onto a cold tile floor; the struggle is real. We have explored how tile came to be the bathroom floor covering of choice, but how are we solving the cold footie problem?

Radiant Floor Heating

I know heated flooring sounds a bit posh, but it isn't as expensive as it sounds. Radiant flooring is energy-efficient. As long as you say *energy-efficient* <u>before</u> a dollar sign, it's okay to spend the money. That's the rule.

<u>Radiant</u> floor heating is like having the warmth of that beloved 70s space heater on your feet and resonating throughout the room. There are two different types of energy-efficient floor heating:

- Electric - Wiring under the floor is heated.
- Water-based - Hot water runs through pipes under the floor creating heat.

The science behind this is pretty simple; heat rises. We use this scientific gem to harness the power of heat upward. By heating from the floor up, the heat flow is optimized in your house. *Boom.*

What makes radiant flooring energy efficient is that radiators generally need to reach heights of 149 to 167 degrees Fahrenheit to heat a room. However, depending on your floor finish, radiant floor heating only needs to sit at 84 degrees Fahrenheit or *less.* Guess what that does to utility bills? It lowers them 15%; I looked it up.

Have you ever sat across the room from a heating vent shivering in your blankie and waiting for the heat to get to you? Or moved the couch to the perfect place under the heating vent to comfortably watch TV while your kids freeze on the other side of the room? You can't even go pee for fear of losing your cozy spot. When you have radiant floor heating, the entire floor surface is heated. Heat is distributed evenly throughout the room.

Other radiant flooring benefits are:

- A 30-year warranty
- Requires virtually no maintenance
- Works with Smart Wifi thermostat or standard

- Works with all floor coverings: carpet, wood, tile, vinyl - there is no limit
- Better air quality than other heating methods

How much does it cost? Cost depends on the material and vendor you select. You can expect the cost to range from $10 to $12 per square foot (about $600 for a remodeling project). Of course, the more custom the job, the higher the price will go.

The average bathroom is about 20 to 146 square feet, so let's take the mid-size of a 50 square foot bathroom. Depending on what you select, the cost could be as low as $265. A larger master bathroom of 120 square feet would be about $600 to $800. Redoing your entire house with radiant flooring may take a bit of disciplined budgeting if you're into that sort of thing. On the other hand, the decline in cost of utilities may convert you from bathroom rugs to elegant, energy-efficient (remember to say that), radiant heated floors.

Bathroom Rugs

It's something your grandma did; stop it.

CHAPTER 2

Carpeted Kitchens & Dining Rooms, That's A Hard No!

When I was growing up, we celebrated Thanksgiving at my Great-Great Grandmother's house. According to the women in my family, *the women live forever because we have grit and a good sense of humor.* If you ask the men, *the women kill the men off early with that humor.* Anyway, Grams had a beautiful dining room and kitchen; both carpeted.

Grams invested in large plastic sheets (now that I think about it, it straight-up may have been Reynolds Plastic Wrap) under the dining room table and a plastic runway that sprawled from the dining room to the basement door protecting the luscious shag carpet. The plastic aesthetics made the interior look like a prep-room for Dexter or the lair of an all-girls mud wrestling team.

The plastic pathways were our walking areas. Grams refused children cups of water until we sat criss-cross-applesauce on the designated plastic areas. When she passed on, Thanksgiving was moved to my Aunt's house. My Aunt also had a large lovely carpeted dining room. However, she thought it was silly to drape plastic over a pristine carpet. There's that humor again. At my Aunt's house, if food dropped on the floor, everyone had to:

1. Stop eating
2. Evacuate the table in an orderly fashion
3. Watch the womenfolk attack the stain and cheer them on

The drill had been rehearsed and perfected. Only when the stain was remedied could we sit back down to Thanksgiving dinner under the raptor-style glare of my Aunt, who would lose her shit if anything else was dropped. I particularly enjoyed passing the cranberry mold across the table with a shaky hand and watching her nostrils flare in anticipation. Did I mention kids younger than 12 ate in the garage at a fold-out table? My family builds character.

What I am pointing out here is that the form of a room should fit its function. If it doesn't, you stress yourself out in the unrelenting battle of bending function into form. It's simply not practical. As a tenacious youth, I would never tire of amplifying the fear of falling food to see my Aunt react. She's lucky we didn't have cell phones because it would be on YouTube in slow motion. I was terrible.

Payback is indeed a bitch because Thanksgiving is now at *my* house, on *my* lovely ceramic tile floor. The most stress my family is subjected to is lifting their feet or suffering the consequences of being man-handled as my little Rumba passes by. The payback is the dirty dishes; I despise doing dishes. If I thought I could get away with it, I would use paper plates but the lecturing that would ensue isn't worth it. You choose your pain, you know?

The Insanity of Kitchen & Dining Room Carpets

We established that hippies are responsible for indulging in shag carpeting for bathrooms, kitchens, walls, and van dashboards. The Post-WWII era got things started with tightly woven carpets. Those loose, big shag carpets - all 70s, baby. During the 70s, the TV transformed from black and white to color. Color TV launched a new platform to experience colors in new ways across American homes. Orange was the new black and gray.

With the revolutionary wave of color, nylon carpets took a spin on the palette and produced carpets in *every* color. Nylon carpet was considered practical and attractive for kitchens and dining rooms. The words *practical* and *kitchen carpet* don't belong in the same thought. Everything that has to do with *mess* and *perishable* is located in one convenient place, the kitchen. Any carpet exacerbates this volatile situation.

The kitchen houses the appliances necessary to prepare, store, and eat food. The dining room serves the *explicit* function of dining on food, usually with guests. So, how in the holy hell is a carpet of any kind going to enhance the function of those rooms? For examples see: (https://clickamericana.com/topics/home-garden/kitchen-carpet-for-people-who-dont-like-kitchen-carpet-1968)

As a type of solution, people recently settled for placing rugs in the kitchen and under dining room tables to accent their homes and show their interior design prowess. These are still carpets but better than full coverage. How many times do you clean those rugs a day? It's best to break the habit of rugs before you spend a mint in replacing them when soiled, which is more often than you think. The National Center for Healthy Housing has written an official statement to avoid placing carpets in <u>kitchens</u>; let me enlighten you on why carpets, rugs, and food do not mix.

The Disturbing Reality Of Food & Carpet

Carpet attracts *and* acts as a catch-all <u>filter</u> for daily life. Dirt, grime, and bacteria can't resist the carpet's mating calls, and it builds up - FAST. There is a time when this dirt and debris carpet mating fills the carpet to capacity. When the carpet is 'full', it can no longer 'filter'. When the carpet can no longer filter, all the residue of life and food pile on top of the fibers. These filthy particles sit menacingly and wait for an appointment with a professional cleaning. If you vacuum the top layer, the carpet is still full. The particles continue building up and lurking across carpet fibres. *Particles* is a sugar-coated name for:

- Skin cells (both human and animal)
- Air pollutants (including pollen, fungi, and chemicals)
- Bacteria
- Cigarette smoke
- Tars

Yummy right? Here's the real kick in the pants, dust mites are a thing.

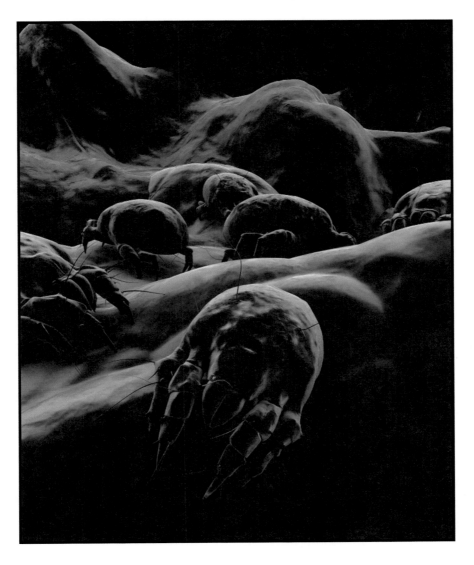

Dust mites are tiny, evil insects. Dust mite droppings exacerbate conditions of people with allergies and asthma. Dust mites LOVE particles and eat flakes of dead skin and pet dander trapped in the carpet as well as carpet fibers. Food crumbs decay and become dust and bacteria. When food decays, the aroma serves as the dinner bell to cockroaches. It's a really twisted Pavlov's dog dynamic. These pests salivate for carpet treats.

It's not the stains you need to worry about; it's the party of insects invited to infest your carpet. Since your carpet acts as a filter, it absorbs and pulls in particles; how do you think that correlates with food droppings? Vacuuming your carpet twice a week isn't good enough to remove these particles either, just so you know. The question then becomes: *What is an alternative to carpet in the kitchen and dining room?*

The Alternatives To Carpeted Kitchens & Dining Rooms

Technology in the kitchen floor space has come a long way in the past few years. However, the wood-look has always been a classic and continues to trend; it is evergreen. Let's be clear; it is the *wood-look* that is popular in kitchen flooring, not *actual* wood. Actual wood requires demanding maintenance and defeats the purpose of a low-maintenance, durable, practical kitchen floor.

Waterproof Vinyl Kitchen Flooring

Vinyl flooring has evolved in leaps and bounds in popularity across American kitchens and dining rooms because it is:

- Resilient
- Versatile
- Economical
- Trendy
- 100% waterproof

Vinyl flooring is the Mystique of the <u>flooring</u> world. If you don't know who Mystique is (and subsequently geeking out with me right now), she is a Marvel Comic character in X-Men. Mystique can shift her biological cells to change her appearance and assume any form, human or animal - even her voice changes. Cool, right? Vinyl kitchen flooring has this superpower.

If you want wood, vinyl flooring takes the form of wood. Vinyl flooring is a chameleon and can look like tile, ceramic, stone, leather, and whatever other texture you like. What's excellent is vinyl flooring gives you the *look* without the cost or maintenance of the real thing. In addition, vinyl doesn't sacrifice its durability in taking on any of these different forms and is usually a fraction of the cost.

Another cool feature of vinyl flooring is it is not a cold type of flooring. If you don't have radiant flooring, Vinyl flooring is the next best option because it is relatively warm to stand on and, get this - glassware often doesn't break when it's dropped. Science is cool.

Vinyl doesn't stain, scratch, or fade, so it can handle a busy household full of kids and pets. Vinyl flooring also features a layer of antimicrobial protection. This means vinyl flooring fights off bacteria, mold, and mildew - something a carpeted kitchen or dining room can't do. Cleaning vinyl is easy. Going over the surface with a damp mop or cloth is all it takes. Vinyl has four layers:

- Protective Urethane top
- Clear Vinyl layer
- Printed design layer
- Felt or fiberglass backing

Vinyl flooring can be purchased in sheets, tiles, or planks, depending on the look you want to emulate in your kitchen. You can easily install it yourself. The national <u>average</u> for customizing your floor with vinyl is about $1,800, depending on your choice, making it the most durable, practical, and best option for your dollar. Vinyl flooring lasts about 20 years and has proven to be well worth the investment.

CHAPTER 3

Fuck Blinds: Why No One-Way Windows?

Crime shows often highlight a handcuffed suspect sitting in a metal chair being grilled by a clever detective with superior intellect and mastery skills in intimidation. The detective flawlessly extracts the criminal's confession and gives a wink and confident smile to the one-way glass separating the interrogation room from the audience on the other side. After seeing this spectacle, our inner voice whispers; a *one-way mirror would be sexy in my living room.*

Can I Get One-Way Glass?

According to the laws of <u>physics</u>, the simple answer is *no, you can't have a one-way mirror.* One-way glass doesn't exist. However, the *illusion* of one-way glass <u>does</u> exist with one tiny inconvenient detail. An important detail if you like to walk around your home wearing nothing but a smile.

A one-way mirror is glass with a reflective coating or film that plays with available light sources. The side of the glass that is lit will allow you to see your reflection - like looking in a mirror. In contrast, the dark side of the glass allows you to see through the glass, like looking through a window into a suspect interrogation room.

The glass interacting with the light is why the viewing room in those crime shows is dark. The dark side can see the interrogation room, but the lit up interrogation room can't see the viewing room. If the viewing room turned on the light, the magic of the light source would dissipate, and the power of the one-way glass would cease to exist.

Now, pull that theory into your home. When the sun is up, the exterior of your house is full of light. Therefore, you would be able to see outside while no one can look inside your windows. However, as night approaches and the light source changes from sun to interior lighting, it is time to put on pants because people can see through your windows while you look at your reflection.

It's a small detail, but an important one, unless you are into that sort of thing (let your freak flag fly). The answer then becomes *yes*; you can achieve a one-way mirror, or privacy window, effectively for all the windows in your house. Doing so has a plethora of advantageous features. If you decide to implement a one-way glass effect, there are a few choices.

One-Way Window Glass

One-way window glass is reflective on one side and transparent on the other. This is a more costly option than tinted one-way windows. This option closely resembles the glass you see in interrogation rooms (not that I would know; that's my story and I'm sticking to it). The most significant benefit of glass instead of tint is the durability. <u>Glass</u> won't:

- Fade
- Peel
- Scratch; and
- Has a longer lifespan

These benefits justify the extra cost in the long run for some. The catch is that this kind of glass is a specialty product provided by a select few retailers. You, of course, do get the bragging rights to say you have the most sophisticated 'police approved' glass windows, which is a definite flex point.

One-way glass usually costs about $150 to $300 for 100 square <u>meters</u>. That's right; I said *meters* because it is a specialty glass and can be found only at a few select vendors in the US and <u>overseas</u>. It is much easier and cheaper to spring for the film.

One-Way Window Film

There is a one-way window film that allows you to secure privacy during the daytime for all of your windows. Film has the added benefit of filtering the natural light inside. This film applies a reflective cover to one side of the glass.

The most significant benefit of one-way film is it is a fraction of the cost of glass, making it ideal for residential homes. The installation process is simple too. It is installed like any other window film, so it can be a DIY project. You just need to put the adhesive (sticky side) right to the glass. This makes it easy to 'uninstall' too if you mess up and need the pros to do it. Some of the other advantages of window film are:

- Rejects heat (up to 82%)
- Minimizes glare (up to 93%)
- Filters UV rays (about 99%)

The downside of film is that it isn't going to have the durability of glass, but it is also easy to replace.

DotView Is The Bomb In One-Way Windows

Now, if you want to get fancy and roll like a baller, invest in <u>DotView</u>. DotView (McGrory Glass) has the options of an opaque surface, decorative color, or graphic image on one side with the tint on the opposite side. Having these options allows you to personalize your house. DotView has:

- Solar control
- One-Way vision graphics
- Privacy & Security features

And it is just plain fanfukintastic. The solar control options can be enhanced with low-emissivity coatings reducing glare and heat for energy efficiency and comfort while having complete visibility outside. The decorative part is fantastic because they can add:

- Color
- Logos
- Images
- Text
- Designs
- Graphics

All without being seen from the inside. This means if you have a big bay living room window, you could put any design or wording you wanted to on it to be seen from the outside. If you want to make the neighbors wonder, you can put *I'M NOT WEARING PANTS* in big red letters viewed by the public at large *without* seeing these letters on your window from the inside; all you would see is light. DotView offers security with 30,000 psi of tensile strength to the already penetration-resistant glass. To simplify the technical jargon, the windows have the structure and ample force to hold out during hurricane winds.

How Much Does Window Tinting Cost

As with most things, you get what you pay for. The premium window tints will have more energy-saving features, longer shelf life, and, yes, be more expensive. It is hard to nail down exactly how much window tinting will cost because of the variety of products and manufacturers out there, but here is a rough idea:

- The Bare Necessity Film: $8-$10/square foot
- Middle Ground: $11-$14/square foot
- The High Roller $15+/square foot

You should expect anywhere from $750 to $5,000 when doing a window tinting refurbishment for your home. The installation is fast, usually one day, taking about 15 minutes per window. Higher or odd-shaped windows will run you a little more.

How Long Does Window Tinting Last

The quality of the film you choose will have the most significant impact on how long it lasts. DotView will probably last twice as long as competitors because it isn't a perforated film and it's high quality glass. Overall, you can expect 5 to 30 years with decent quality, installation, and maintenance.

CHAPTER 4

Laundry Belongs Upstairs

The ritual begins with collecting laundry strewn all over the upstairs and awkwardly balancing the overloaded bundle on our hip; because, let's face it, two trips are for pussies. Next, we bob and weave obstacles we can't see and navigate near-death experiences between the stairs and the laundry room.

Our acrobatic ninja skills and misguided determination to avoid tripping over the cat on the very last stair are followed by unceremoniously hurling the load into the washer. Perhaps you've cussed the old familiar words or made up a few new ones along the way, but at some point, you lost the battle and yelled in frustration- *Why isn't the laundry room upstairs*!

It's not like we need to wash our clothes in the stream and beat them against rocks anymore, at least not for a few centuries. In a 2-story home, you would think the washer and dryer would have found themselves on the second story by now. To figure out the present, we often have to look at the past, so let's start with the bloody Romans.

How The Romans Did Laundry

Romans took clean laundry seriously. They should take it seriously for the amount of toga they wrapped themselves in throughout the day. Romans were known for changing their attire for daily events, and Romans liked to party. Roman fullers (professional toga cleaners) would handle toga washing, drying, and dying and were paid handsomely for doing so, with one minor caveat.

Mind you; soap was not invented until the 19th century. Who needs soap when you have human urine collected from public restrooms? Read that again; I will give that a moment to soak in.

Human urine contains ammonia and was used as a cleaning agent for several things. Human urine was called chamber-lye. Chamber-lye sounds prettier than urine. Sometimes it's all about presentation. Chamber-lye could:

- Remove stains
- Dissolve grease
- Loosen dirt
- Bleach yellowing fabrics (ironic, isn't it?)

Interesting, but absolutely no bearing on how laundry rooms moved into the house; Romans are just fantastic to talk about. Back to business.

Thor: The Master Of Laundry

The Industrial Revolution paved the way for an indoor laundry room with plumbing and electricity access to every home. However, during that period, washboards and manually cranked wooden drum DIY projects served as the primary way to wash clothes.

The Shakers in Pennsylvania mastered wooden washing machines and designed them to work on a commercial scale. These behemoth washers were displayed at the Centennial <u>Exposition</u> in Philadelphia in 1876. But, still not our culprit.

Then there was Thor, great name, right? Most commercial appliances were powered by steam, which wasn't ideal for the home. Alva Fisher invented Thor, a commercial beast of a washing machine, for Hurley Machine Company of Chicago in 1908. It came to life with electricity, not steam. Thor was the turning point that started to move the washer inside the American home.

Laundry Makes It Into The Home

By <u>1937</u>, the household-size electric washing machine came onto the market and was followed by the tumble dryer a year later. At this point, America looked at the rooms in their house and noticed they didn't have a laundry room. Until a room could be designed, washers and dryers went where all the other appliances were stored; the kitchen.

The washing machines were deafening at the time, so homes built after World War II reserved basements for the laundry room's prominent location. The space worked to contain the commotion under the house, muting noise from living spaces.

In the 1970s (yep, hippies, I knew it), homes became larger to accommodate all of the technological advances that had taken place. With the washing machines being quieter, laundry rooms were moved onto the main floor, usually combined with mudrooms linked to the garage.

Reasons Why Laundry Rooms Are On The Main Floor

There have been several reasons stated to me and across the internet as to *why* the laundry room is on the first floor of a two-story home when the bedrooms are upstairs. If the master bedroom is downstairs, I can see the reason for the laundry room on the main floor, but then the question just floats to, *why not two laundries*? But, let's not get ahead of ourselves.

Reason One: Social Value

One popular reason for a main floor laundry room is people like to socialize. People feel they are missing something if they are upstairs doing laundry, isolated, while the family is downstairs having fun. Is a family that fun on a weekday night? If so, I'm doing it wrong. Although I'm not opposed to a reality show in a laundry mat setting, I think this justification for putting the laundry on the main floor for quality time is stretching it.

Reason Two: Multi-Tasking Ability

Another reason that I was given is that it is easier to include laundry tasks with other household duties by locating the washer and dryer on the main floor. Overcooked meatloaf won't happen because you are right there watching the oven while tending to the laundry. You can whisk around and straighten up the house while waiting for the laundry timer to go off. Stop it.

No one sits and looks at the washing machine spin. Well, not for the entire duration anyway. The machines come equipped with severely ear-piercing buzzers or rocking bell tunes to notify you it's time for 'the change.'

Reason Three: Expense

Expense is a pretty good reason. If you are living in a two-story home that has been prebuilt, you may not be willing to expend the <u>funds</u> to put the laundry room on the second floor with:

- Plumbing costs for water and drain lines
- Electrician costs for outlets and light fixtures
- Insulation costs to neutralize noise
- Structural costs to reinforce the floors; and
- Contractor for cabinets and countertops

This cost averages $14,825 to move the laundry room upstairs and equip it with all the bells and whistles. If the price has a comma in it, it requires a lively discussion with the spouse on which kid you are booting from the house or moving into the closet to free up their room for the laundry room. This is frowned upon in my household. Ask me how I know.

Reason Four: Multipurpose Functionality On The Main Floor

People have recently started refurbishing laundry rooms to multipurpose room combos like:

- Laundry/Office
- Laundry/Playroom
- Laundry/Craft Area
- Laundry/Workspace
- Laundry/Greenhouse

Depending on what you are doing, for just the laundry room refurbishment, the average cost is around $8,000. Add the office or workspace costs, and you quickly meet or exceed the cost of moving the room upstairs.

The only difference here is, there is likely more room on the first floor to orchestrate a double room by cashing in the formal dining room in exchange for laundry room real estate; I mean, who uses dining rooms anyway? Aren't we all eating in front of the TV on TV trays? For example see: (https://dreamhousestudios.net/)

Reason Five: The Senior Reason

There will come a time when we are older, those upstairs rooms are empty, and our lack of mobility requires a laundry room on the first floor. Honestly, probably time to invest in a one-story where laundry rooms on the main floor make sense.

Why Not A Laundry Chute?

When I was young, I would visit my Aunt's house. The place was full of things I was not allowed to touch. The home was a living museum and smelled like lavender. It was unnatural and in direct opposition to my mom's house that usually smelled like a crockpot meal. I determined the reason for the polar opposite aromas was that my Aunt had a laundry chute in her house and my mom didn't.

Laundry chutes hide our dirty little secrets and not just the smelly, sweaty sock variety. Laundry chute design has been used for beer, the Manhattan Project, and hospitals. Laundry chutes were also great for <u>hiding</u> the occasional spoils from a robbery, providing an escape for patients in an asylum, or hiding a dead body. People have even been known to get stuck in them and be found months later. Google laundry chutes and you will find plenty of macabre stories. Frankly, none of these overpower my need to *not* haul laundry up and down stairs.

While Googling, I was pleasantly surprised to find instructional videos on chute installation and chute kits. Installing a laundry chute is inexpensive, relatively easy, and can be a DIY project. Luckily, preventative measures can be taken to thwart children from shoving family pets into the chute or going tumbling down themselves. Kids that don't know better tend to be height-challenged (short). Placing a laundry chute entrance where they can't reach it is ideal. If you are extremely paranoid, or have egregiously unruly children, combination locks or other such obstacles will suffice as child proofing. Yes, I am that lazy. Laundry chutes in a two-story house costs under $2,000 in most cases.

Generally, you want to install a chute directly above, or close to, the laundry room. The idea is to have clothes drop in a basket close to the washer. There are mechanisms that will suck laundry from about 8 different rooms. Yes, you read that right. The <u>Laundry Jet Plus</u> is your solution. It installs inside cabinetry so it's hidden and fits the laundry room aesthetics. The vacuum power is impressive, but it's not what stole my heart. The Laundry Jet Plus has a RETURN UNIT Option. This sends your *clean* clothes back to the bedroom or wherever. Three words: Sign. Me. Up. For example see:

<u>https://www.katahdincedarloghomes.com/blog/laundry-jet/</u>

If you require a simple chute, it is relatively easy to do it yourself. According to <u>Fine HomeBuilding</u>, the best size for a laundry chute is 12 x 12 inches. The goal is to keep the chute smooth to avoid snags and clothes getting stuck. Metal ductwork usually does the trick and it's easy to angle and work with. The benefits of installing a chute are immediate.

Laundry Rooms & Bedrooms

It is practical to have a laundry room near the location of your walk-in closets, dressers, and drawers where your clothes are stored, no? Bedrooms are the intimate, secluded places where we pause by the full-length mirror to critique ourselves before abruptly changing what we are wearing to look presentable in public. Standing in front of a mirror before leaving the house may not apply to some of the Walmart late-night shoppers I have seen. But then again, some of those shoppers stood in front of the mirror and declared, *Damn! I look good!* as they walked out the door. Beauty is in the eye of the beholder.

Think of how much time could be saved if we could walk a few steps and toss a dirty load of clothes in for washing. No more scurrying room to room picking up clothes from the floor because children are violently allergic to hampers. Gone are the days of the *find the smell* game.

Having a laundry room near the bedroom promotes a minimum amount of laundry done during the week to avoid the mountains of clothes springing up on the weekends. As a result, you can allocate your time better and leave an opening for more quality time and things you *want* to do. Efficient time management puts you back in the driver's seat as master of your destiny.

Today's families do not circulate firmly around the mother holding down the household. Instead, they are filled with teens that need to do their laundry with specific outfits for sports and clubs. Having a laundry room near the bedrooms allows everyone to be self-sufficient and have accountability for their items. This is Adulting 101.

Keeping the laundry upstairs means your downstairs will stay tidier and organized without the baskets of folded laundry scattered across living room furniture. This saves embarrassing undergarment peeps by the neighbor dropping in unannounced. Also, a laundry room upstairs is cheaper than moving; some things you just can't unsee.

CHAPTER 5

Balconies: Real or Fake? & Why Attics?

Juliet balconies, French balconies, or Balconettes are not interchangeable. We are not talking about the huge beautiful balconies, we are talking about the little suicide slab outside a window. Juliet balconies are considered a decorative element perched on the exterior of a high window. The appendage is usually wrapped in iron. If you open the window, you can't put both feet out for lack of room. It is a *false* balcony, the little liar. False balconies do come with a wild history that transformed into romantic notions which made them popular in today's American designs.

When I say romantic notion, I am speaking of Romeo and Juliet (hence the Juliet balcony name) where she called to him from her high window. So endearing was this scene that the Balconette <u>Bra</u> is named after the architectural highlight to serve as a balcony for breasts. The bras feature less material and have provided an uplifting experience for stars like Marilyn Monroe who's bubbling bounty supported her to fame and fandom.

Wild History Of The Balconette

It is true that the Balconette started in France, but back then, it was more than decoration and served a distinct purpose. During the Middle Ages, rampant unsanitary conditions flourished, and people had extremely odd and obscenely incorrect ideas of what caused illness.

The Paris population (as well as most of Europe, let's be real) believed there was no connection between everyone inhabiting an apartment or home using the same bucket as a communal toilet and hurling the contents out the window when finished. Out of sight, out of mind. To them, this bucket hurling was inconsequential on public wellness. Walking down the streets of Paris required a quick pace and a duck and cover scurry for a few reasons:

- The smell was so thick it would stick to you
- A flying turd may hit you

Paris streets got so bad that in 1270, the government thought they may need to do something about the outpouring. I mean, people were beginning to talk. The government put their foot down (deep) and prohibited anyone from casting human waste buckets out the window. Those caught doing so would be severely fined. Unfortunately, it is pretty easy not to get caught. Once waste splats on the pavement, it's everyone's poo. Kind of like who owns the fart in an elevator. Fast forward a century later, and people were still hurling their biscuits out the window.

Unable to detour the public atrocity from occurring, the French government philosophy was *if you can't beat 'em, maybe we give them a conditional.* The government approved public waste being hurled from windows under one condition: You must cry, *"Beware, I'm pouring!"* thrice (3 times). Yup, that should do it; check that box. A warning became common courtesy for sewage wars.

How does this relate to Balconettes? Mind you; this was the whole population of Paris (and Europe) participating in this practice. It wasn't limited to common folk. *Population* includes royalty, noblemen, the Louvre (wow!) and the poor alike. However, the rich, for even more convenience than tossing a bucket out the window, thought of a new method. And here I didn't think you could get more lazy or disgusting.

Large floor to ceiling windows started being built in the wealthier homes with no sills and guardrails wrapped on the exterior, the poop stoop. With these fantastic features, one could simply lean out the window without fear of falling and handle business, no need to touch a nasty bucket for a barbaric turd toss.

This waste disposal process was much more refined. The hands could stay clean and you could get right back to the party on the inside of the window. Yes, this was a party favor, not a party foul. Fun fact, the curved shape that the balconette has highlighted throughout the years was developed for ease of squatting with grip rails. Innovation is fantastic. Clearly, there was enough room to stand and manuever a release of waste on a Balconette, so, how did the suicide ledge make it into American architectural design?

The Prestige Of Juliet Balconies

When the original purpose was taken away from the French balcony, the Europeans took over and glorified balconies during the 18th and 19th centuries. Balconies transitioned from privies to a sign of sophistication, elegance, and grandeur - quite a different take from an outdoor toilet.

Britain's Regency Era was full to the brim with romanticism and extravagance. This time period coincided with falling iron prices making iron easy to obtain. Iron was soon crafted into elaborate designs enclosing large windows in an embrace.

A balconette on the exterior of a home was a badge of prestigious, luxuriant living and came to be seen as an architectural staple. Juliet balconies allowed you to open the doors inward and let light and fresh air flood the room gushing from the floor to ceiling windows.

Popularity Of Juliet Balconies In America

The popularity of Juliet balconies crossed over the ocean primarily by pop culture, making them the epitome of stature and wealth. Juliet balconies have set magnificent stages of grandeur in:

- Royal addresses: Royal highness waving to the adoring crowd
- Pop waves: Famed actors and musicians making appearances on hotel stoops
- Cruise cabins: You upgrade to the Juliet balcony suite to wave to the crowd and have a scenic view
- Movie moments: Evita's glorious and moving scene of Eva Peron's address to Argentina

Juliet balconies provided a connection from the crowd to those perched on the balcony, exuding empowerment and godliness. Pop culture helped romanticize the Juliet balcony across several countries. The phenomenon led to homeowners seeking these grandiose platforms encased in decorative wrought iron to add spice to an otherwise dull and bland home exterior. Juliette balconies are used to add dimension and ventilation to vertical spaces that do not have the luxury of adding a full balcony, such as this New York condo. For example see: https://streeteasy.com/blog/

Juliette balconies are an inexpensive way to enhance space and, in most cases, do not require a special building permit. In fact, it is the balcony that allows for the wide door and not a small window. Note the floor to ceiling sliding glass. What several Americans have pasted on the outside of homes across windows do not qualify as Juliet balconies.

You Have Been Fauxed

The key features of a Juliet Balcony are:

- Floor to ceiling windows
- Doors that open inward
- Elaborate railing with a foot of space on the balcony

Faux balconies have no platform and, more than likely, no functional doors or windows.

Faux balconies are spreading across the US like wildfire. Faux balconies serve as elaborate house jewelry with zero purpose. Well, zero meaningful purposes. It is something for pigeons to nest on or precariously loop some Christmas lights over.

Due to faux balconies' relatively inexpensive and easy to install nature, people can afford them. But think about it, developers install these faux balconies *before* you purchase your home. You didn't actually go through the faux balcony catalog and buy the exalted jail window yourself.

Developers decided these bars provide instant street credit connected with old-world prestige and beauty- yeah, fuck those guys, give us the real thing. Faux balconies cost about $1,000 uninstalled. Let's say you have 4 windows on the second floor, that's $4,000. I can live like royalty for a week in Jamaica with $4,000. In my mind, this unnecessarily inflates the cost of the home. Give us a rebate or give us the damn balcony, devs.

Faux balconies are designed to draw attention to the outside of your home and be the first thing you see. We should take a minute to discuss what should be seen immediately when you enter a front door.

Benches By Front Doors Are Mandatory

When you walk into the entryway of someone's home, your eyes immediately dart around for the shoe pile to determine if it is a shoeless house. If it is, you get the privilege of hopping on one foot awkwardly to keep your balance in an effort to prevent your hand from touching their walls. Once you remove one shoe, the process starts over again of looking like a jackass as you try to keep your balance to remove the other shoe and add them to the snow-crusted melting heap of shoes by the door.

Entryways should be equipped with a place to store shoes and coats easily to save guests from interpreting the house rules. Period. Now, back to things homes don't need besides those faux balconies.

Attics - Just, Why?

Flowers In The Attic is a gothic novel released in 1979, written by VC Andrews as the first book in a demented series (way more sinister than the twinkling vampires that have girls hearts all aflutter). VC Andrews is the author that launched my love of reading and horror flicks during my teen years. No, it wasn't Steven King. I do love his horror, but it is abrupt and tangible whereas Andrews puts things in your head to simmer and grapple with the psychological sickness. This may be why the book was banned due to child abuse and incest storylines. As with most disturbing things, pop culture adopted and resurrected it.

The series served as my first real glimpse of attics. Movies and books from different authors continued to inflate the perpetual evil connotations of attics. Attics were places harboring dusty, dangerous discoveries and shameful family secrets. I stayed away from attics in the midwest because it was inevitable I would be lured into some peril by evil spirits inhabiting the attic walls (Amityville Horror windows didn't help). It did get me thinking, though, why do we need attics? Or do we?

A Bit Of History On Attics

Older homes have more extensive attics (500 square feet or more). The larger attics can be made into extra bedrooms, offices, or playrooms. Most attics are left unfinished and converted into cozy living spaces later by new owners.

Before 1950s homebuilding, large attics were prominent because of the thousand-year-old concept of using large rafters to support a roof. When builders switched to roof trusses, the attics became more like a crawl space filled with insulation.

A few things were going on during this time. Homes were getting bigger, and basement waterproofing was getting better. With better headspace in basements, storage began to migrate that way. Having an attic depends on where you live; if you don't have a basement due to poor soil, you will likely have an attic.

Colder climates tend to have pitched roofs to drain water and snow off the roof to avoid roof damage. It is recommended in those areas to <u>seal</u> off the attic, ventilate it, and have it insulated for energy efficiency. Unless your attic can look like this:

There is really no point in having one, is there?

How To Get Rid Of An Attic

If you have a small attic, and the framework of the roof is rafters, creating vaulted ceilings is a definite possibility because the roof stays intact. With trusses, it is an expensive, complicated process that may not be worth it.

Vaulting your ceilings may lead to more energy costs because you are removing insulation and adding more height to the room for aesthetics. On average, it costs about $60 per square foot to lift the ceiling.

Do Attics Have A Purpose?

If your attic isn't at least 500 square feet, it is a waste of space and has no real value. It may be easier and more cost-effective to seal it like an Egyptian tomb and keep the mystery alive.

CHAPTER 6

WTF is this Room & Soundproof Your Shit

Homes come equipped with basic standards for a majority of Americans. The main recipe for a home is: kitchen, bathroom, living room, and bedroom which can be decorated and customized at your leisure. Other features and rooms run on a sliding scale of what one can afford to build.

Then there are those homes that have rooms...and rooms....and more rooms and you have no idea what they are for. For example, in my hometown, there is a historic home that was turned into a museum of sorts. A testament to what the past looked like in this small town of 30,000. People book it for weddings, family photos, and the like.

Each school year, we were filed into the home and taken on a tour to educate us about our past and how far we have crawled up the home building evolutionary ladder. There were at least 20 rooms in this home labeled with formal, usually foreign, names. For example see: https://www.lasr.net/travel/city.php?Louis+E.+May+Historical+Museum&TravelTo=NE0109007&VA=Y&Attraction ID=NE0109007a002

It was cool and surprisingly easy to get lost in because the rooms were small, like office cubicles which made it rather maze-ish. The point is, there are rooms in homes, especially older homes, that have all these extra formal rooms and I still don't know what to call them. As a public service to prevent awkward moments at family homes and school tours, I did some homework to enlighten us on room etiquette in old homes.

The Parlor

Parlors are set-apart rooms at the entryway of a home and elaborately decorated. This was the trophy room of the house, the pride of the family, where they would showcase items from faraway places and monumental achievements.

Women were responsible for lavishing their attention and the family fortune on the Parlor to create an experience, not just a passive room, for their guests. The appearance of the room was a statement of the family's hierarchy in the world and stature in the community.

One of the more interesting things about Parlors is they not only hosted celebrated events like weddings, but they also hosted intimate funerals. Death was held close to the home's bosom. Most people in historical times were cared for and died in the home.

During the Victorian era, it was not uncommon for people to pose with the deceased to have a memento of their time together in the family home. It was custom that generations would occupy the home throughout their lives - meaning there were several funerals held in Parlors over the years. Birth, life, and death revolved around the home.

We weren't the only culture participating in the tradition of bringing a dead body into the home. In some cases, Americans were on the conservative side of death. The Famadihana, better known as Turning of the Bones, now there's a party. The Malgasy people celebrate the Famadihana by taking a family trip to the cemetery, digging up graves, dousing the decomposing corpses with perfume, wrapping the remains in silk, and bringing the party home.

This sets off every alarm of psychological imbalance and traumatization in my body, but to each his own, right? The Malgasy dance, sing songs, talk to the fleshy mass, and break out the red solo cups of fun. They believe until the body is fully decomposed, spirits dwell between this world and the next - riveting. Our Parlor festivities pale in comparison.

Back to business, the Parlor is where funeral parlors get their name. Having funerals in the home Parlor was commonplace until the high bodycount of the Civil War made home funerals impractical and created the first funeral homes. The formal, luxurious, uncomfortable furniture in the residential home could only accommodate so many people and transporting bodies exposed to the elements without preservation ... well, we might as well be Malgasy. No one wants to see that.

Anyway, formal occasions would be the only time the family and guests used the Parlor. It was one of those untouched rooms - kind of like the sofa your grandma wrapped in plastic to keep pristine. Guests would not see any other portion of the home and would complete their entire stay in the Parlor eating and drinking from the best dish sets the family could afford. The Parlor was meant to be the best of everything--the illusion.

By the 18th century, having a Parlor was a measurement of status. Before there was the picket-fence, suburban American dream; it was the Parlor dream. Parlors represented civilization, sophistication, proper behavior, and the American moxie to go forth and achieve. Parlors were a shrine to validate your family legacy and each generation added to the elite collection contained in the room.

"To the <u>lady of the house</u>, the parlor was, or was supposed to be the expression of her refinement and the stage on which she displayed her breeding, her bibelots, her poise and her culture."

Parlors were the heartbeat in the home. However, with the death room history and decreased use due to functioning and plentiful funeral parlors, Ladies Home Journal made a suggestion in 1910; and it stuck. They stated: *Parlors should be renamed to living rooms to shake off the lingering debris of creepy death photography pics and invite a less morbid tone.*

The goal was to inspire family activities, socialization, and a place for the living to congregate comfortably and happily. Without the stigma of the Parlor, people were far less formal and cold and less likely to harbor insincere pleasantries. People craved the warm, meaningful intimacy of the good life with good friends.

Some people may still have a formal living room for guests and a den or family room for the informal living room. The English language is notorious for being overly complicated by using several words to mean the same thing, just to keep it exciting.

One final note on Parlors, they should not be confused with a foyer. Yes, I confuse them and use them interchangeably.

A *foyer* is the space you step into when you enter a home. Basically, you welcome your guest at the foyer (entryway) and escort them to the Parlor (now living room). Formal, large-scale foyers are reserved for places like hotels where there is public access. Foyers are better known as lobbies.

Fainting Room

Ladies, did you ever go weak in the knees when a virile young man paid you a kindness? Or have you become breathless at the sight of your favorite drummer at a concert? Yeah, me either (sorry, Lars).

Back in the day, women were prone to swooning. So, either we have found our center, or the art of making us swoon has since been vanquished from the earth. If swoon art starts trending again, the Fainting Room may be reinstated.

The Fainting Room was specifically designed for a woman to rest after a fainting spell (pffft). Now granted, I can co-sign on this if a woman's corset was cinched too tight, I have watched Pirates of the Caribbean. These rooms were also popular when women were working through a bit of hysteria. If you don't know what that is, read my <u>blog</u> or listen to my <u>podcast</u>. I am trying to keep this book from going triple-X rated.

Modern Additional Rooms

Today people create a buffet of rooms speaking more to their lifestyle. We tend to bring what requires going outside of the home, into it. For example, why have a gym membership when you have a home gym? Why go play pool when you have a game room with a pool table?

Some believe these extra refinements to the home diminish social interactions with people. Others believe these rooms create a more intimate dynamic by inviting friends to the home to relax. I'm in the middle. Other common additions are:

- Home library
- Sunroom
- Home Bar
- Man Cave
- She Suite
- Craft room
- Home Theater
- Home Office

Personalizing rooms to fit lifestyle is trending and a sustainable contribution to saving you money while celebrating leisure time. Checking in with yourself mentally and identifying ways to enhance the enjoyment of your home is all the rage these days. In the spirit of these renovations, I would like to contribute with a few helpful tips. By tips, I mean unsolicited advice of my personal preferences and pet peeves.

People Who Paint Over Wallpaper

I have a firm belief that people who paint over wallpaper...well, I don't think their cornbread is done in the middle. I once had the thrilling experience of a lifetime when I agreed to renovate an old farm house that had been ordered from a Sears & Roebuck catalogue. YES, they used to do that.

I can't tell you when the house was ordered and delivered to its country road destination, but I can tell you with absolute certainty it had been remodeled at least 17 times before my attempts. I can also tell you it took:

- 17 minutes to get into town and pull into the nearest bar
- 8 minutes to down a beer and a shot
- 7 minutes to the hardware store
- 3 minutes to pet the pig they kept there
- 25 minutes to drive back to the house (I went slower)
- 10 minutes to stare at the house from the car in the driveway and seriously consider burning it down

The home looked similar to the picture above. Words may come to your mind like: *quaint, cute,* or maybe even *charming.* Yeah, don't let the picture fool you, the devil is in the details. This was to be my first home and it had been in the family for as long as anyone could remember. It had also been abandoned for as long as anyone could remember. We partied in it as teenagers and hosted Halloween hay rack rides up and down the country road. At the time, I had no clue I would marry into it and if I had known, I would have avoided the encounter.

My work was cut out for me. I could handle the termites, bugs, vermin, snakes, leaks, graffiti, propane tank, dangerous fouled-up electrical outlet shocks, and hit & miss indoor plumbing. I could even handle the never ending game of 'find the smell' that always ended with a scream, slur of cuss words, and me stomping off to get bleach, gloves, shovel, and a trash can. None of those things enticed me to day drink.

It was the layers of wallpaper and painted over wallpaper in the Parlor (yes, there was a Parlor) which was to be our living room. Armed with a putty knife and a bad attitude, I set to work to find out how much of a chore this first room was going to be. I had already eradicated the road kill and unwelcome house guests.

The coating over these walls was, at a minimum, 5 inches deep in filth, graffiti, wallpaper, and paint. I thought this would take me all day; I was insanely optimistic and naive. Still, I harbored no ill-will against people that painted over wallpaper. That is, until the ***third*** day.

By the 5th day and 8th trip into town for supplies, I had actually struck a match to light this bitch up, but thought better of it and grabbed the hose like it was my lifeline and pulled it into the house. I turned the music up, pushed my goggles down, and flipped the switch on the hose, spraying the walls with water and stripper, while laughing maniacally for an hour.

That was my defining moment. The moment I decided to never layer cake the walls with painted over wallpaper. Yes, eventually I did get the room done. I found out two decades later that steam is the secret weapon. Wallpaper is probably much easier to remove now, especially since most use strippable wallpaper. The moral of the story is don't paint over wallpaper - EVER.

Not Every Room Needs A Closet

Full disclosure for the women of the world, this is not my idea. Do not shoot the messenger. I grew weary of arguing with the co-author on closets. You need to pick your hard in life and arguing this one was not the hard I chose to take on. Closets in every room are a hard 'NO' for the co-author. I say this to prevent my woman card from being revoked. Despite my objections, the man has valid points.

The story begins with why do we have closets? Why do we think we need so many of them? Over the years as more and more houses are built, the closets are not only becoming larger, but we are adding them everywhere in the home.

Let's start with the hallway closets. We don't just need one hallway closet anymore. How about 3? What do we store in these spaces that is so valuable? I will tell you.

Absolutely nothing.

Oftentimes, I will enter someone's home and due to my curious nature, I simply can't help but open doors to find out what's behind them. I find myself hoping to find a secret room full of my greatest desires. Instead, I am greeted with a few rolls of toilet paper, clorox, and 30-year-old bed sheets that the owner simply can't part with. How disappointing. At some point, people need to learn how to throw things away. This brings me to the main culprit: Closets in bedrooms.

In the early 1900's people didn't have closets. They had a large open bedroom to play with and design. Today, closets have preordained where your clothing will be stored. You can't simply change the location of your closet. It's there now. You will never be able to use that wall as a placement for your bed or TV. Nope. That wall is designated for your closet.

It's no small closet either. That closet is probably 10 feet deep and 6 feet wide. Somehow you think you need this. It stores clothing from when you were 15 but now you're 45. You look at it and say,

Well, maybe I can wear this sweater in a year. After my diet, I can try it again. It really is a lovely sweater and I got it on sale!

For the love of all that is holy, THROW IT AWAY! The fact is, if you ever do lose weight, the first thing you will do is go out and celebrate by buying new clothes. As humans, hoarding is instinctual. Hoarding is why closets have become such a large part of our lives. My father's friend built a 20 X 20 shed behind my father's house to store all the junk he has hoarded, erm - *collected*. He probably spent $20,000 on this shed holding a solid $1,000 in junk.

Back to our topic. Closets are notorious for holding items we no longer wear, want, or need. Even if the average person did have this much clothing they use on a daily basis, most of it would take a full year to cycle through. The truth is, as a collective people, we should try to live utilizing *less* clothing. Halting overconsumption and hoarding saves ample space in our homes and reduces hours doing the laundry, costs of the laundry, and probably even helps the environment.

I know. Anxiety flags are popping off in your head and you are screaming on the inside: NO! You are saying to yourself, *I thought this was a chapter about closets*! You are unsettled about me telling you to stop buying so many clothes. Well, they do go hand in hand. Clothes and closets are tied together at the waist if you will.

Let me guess, closets hold your 1985 favorite pair of jeans that you wore to the after school party where you had your first 'moment.' It's time to say goodbye to the past and start looking at utilizing this space for something else.

In the early 1900's, the Armoire was essential in the home. The husband and wife would have dresser drawers and oftentimes have 1 or 2 armoires to store their clothing that required hanging. The beautiful part about an armoire is you can move them into any part of the room at any time. This is great for those that enjoy changing their rooms frequently to create a different space.

Since the early 2000's, this has all changed. Armoires have disappeared and we can't even sell a house without mentioning the luxurious closet space. In today's age, realtors won't consider the room a bedroom without ample closet space. Why can't we just put an Armoire in the back of the room and walla, presto! - complete. Now, you may be sitting here reading this and saying to yourself:

Well, what about all the stuff I DO need? Like these 6 bottles of toothpaste I bought from amazon, or 200 rolls of toilet paper?

OK. I embellish, a little. But seriously, it takes months to go through one bottle of toothpaste. Keep it fresh by buying one at a time. I will give you a pass on the toilet paper though! The truth is, we have other spaces in our house that can store items that are underutilized or simply not used. Let's take a tour through it for a minute.

Most houses have a small closet space that accompanies larger closet space. Small closet space usually lurks under the stairs. The big part of the stairs. What happened to the first 4FT of the stairs as closet space? Surely we can turn this area into storage to store shoes or supplies. Or how about stair drawers?

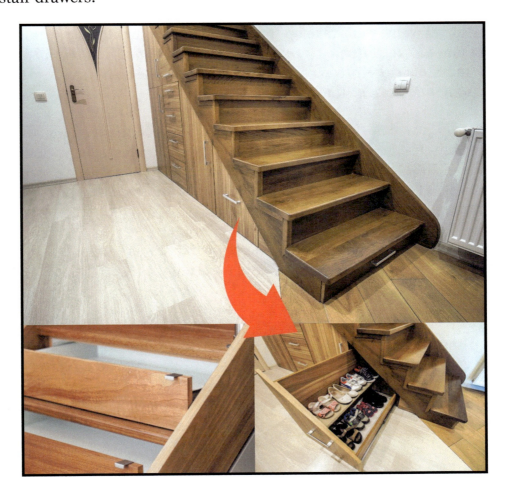

We often don't utilize the space above our cabinets in our kitchen. Or the space in the closet for that matter. Half the closets I open are unorganized junk drawers. A few properly placed tubs or shelfs would make a world of difference (#basketculture). Stop the high school locker insanity.

For those of you with an overwhelming amount of closet space, the first thing that needs to happen is go inside them and start throwing away all those historically archived items from your past. You won't wear it again and honestly the value is minimal. If you think in 50 years it might have value, try to imagine where you will be in 50 years.

Try to think about the space in a different way and how it might look, dare I say (internal gasp) Pinterest? What about walls, walls take up space. The average closet has a 5" thick wall on 2 or three sides. You may say, *well it's just 5 inches or 15 inches total of additional space.* It comes down to, do you need that closet? If you have two closets, can one not be changed to an Armoire? Can you utilize some stair space? Kitchen space?

In my house we did just that. We rebelliously tore down a bedroom closet that was under-designed and then re-designed the closet above the stairs. I am beaming with pride because it felt GOOD. It was LIBERATING. Two simple adjustments and BOOM, we converted the small closet to a walk-in closet and added 30 square feet of space to my room. I replaced the large closet with a 3 X 3 Armoire which maximized space and added 20 sq ft total.

This is important. It's *your* home and in *your* home you want more space. Where will you store the Christmas, Easter, or Halloween decorations? I will tell you.

Not the closet.

If anything, an outdoor shed may actually be the best place for seasonal decor. Sheds hold very little value and are only used 2 to 3 weeks of the year. It's time to start thinking rationally and practically about the items we own and how much we are buying off Amazon. People have a tendency to hoard and over consume - it's our nature. He who dies with the most stuff wins, right?

You never really know how much stuff you have until you buy a new house because you need more space and start packing. When you pack, you start getting rid of half your stuff and wonder how it came to this. Then, you realize you don't need the bigger house, but now you need more stuff to fill it up. It's a vicious cycle. We are grounded by our material possessions, they own us. All those items in your home have to go somewhere when you leave it. And if your family is anything like mine, that's probably the trash can. We touched on space in the stairs, but now, we really need to talk about stairs as a whole.

Stairscapes

I believe in the right tool for every job. When you have a nail, you need a hammer. When you have a screw, you need a screwdriver. When you have carpet, you need a vacuum. When you have hard floors, you need a broom, dustpan, and mop.

We need to cease and desist putting carpet *and* hardwood floors on stairs! One or the other - all carpet or all hardwood. As Highlander said, *"There can be only one."*

Time is the one asset you can never get back. Time turns into a liability quickly if you have to carry twice the tools, up and down stairs. This activity sucks precious energy and time out of your day and your back muscles. I have spent more time than I care to admit being subjected to a half carpeted, half hardwood staircase. It is time abuse and inhumane.

I still have nightmares. Stairs are not wide enough to conveniently set a vacuum on, so you must precariously balance the vacuum, lug it up each stair, and angle the vacuum attachment to properly clean. Then, you need to dust the hardwood spaces and wipe them down. You are essentially doing the job twice.

I am lazy and therefore handle every chore with streamlined efficiency to prevent such a double-chore travesty. No one has time for this. Do yourself a favor and choose one or the other.

Secondly, why stairs? I get that in ancient times stairs were the only way to get to the top, but now? We can either design them better or remove them from the equation. That whole balancing act with the vacuum needs to stop and we need storage space. Why not stairs that are wide enough to accommodate a vacuum? Or at the very least, to set a piece of furniture on that you are moving upstairs.

I thought ramps would be an awesome idea because my Roomba would be able to take care of the cleaning, but swiftly realized I would never be able to stop my children from using it as a slide. Or me. Why not elevators? Residential elevators are about $4,000 and last 20 years with proper maintenance. This more than pays for the time and materials you spend cleaning your stairs. Surprised that someone would want an elevator in their home? It's not as uncommon as you think.

The National Association of Home Builders reports 25% of <u>homeowners</u> desire an elevator in their home. The big question would be the maintenance contract on such an endeavor. Elevators are considered a large appliance and will need routine checks and maintenance schedules. The manufacturer will usually tell you how often it should be serviced and who can service it. Maintenance also depends on where you live. Cities have different safety requirements for residential elevators. Some even require permits.

Most service contracts run between $350 to $1500 per year for residential elevators and come with the installation of diagnostic equipment so the company can look at your elevator and tell what's wrong without being in the room. The benefits of installing an elevator rivals the costs. Elevators elevate your standard of living because you gain a tremendous amount of accessible space. Look at your stairs, now imagine if they weren't there - enough said.

Soundproof Your Shit

The final room I feel we need to address is the bathroom. Yes, I spent a great deal of time on carpeted bathrooms, but I inadvertently left out two key features that should be a requirement in any home. These features contribute to the sanctity of your marriage or add to the blissful oblivion in relationships. They are the bidet and soundproof your bathroom.

Bidets

A few years ago, my family had the opportunity to stay in one of the regal penthouse suites at Red Rock Casino in Las Vegas. The floors were heated, there was an 8-person shower (for what, I could only imagine), lush carpeting and extravagant furniture. But the highlight was the warm toilet seat and welcoming fountain of warm water erupting from the bidet. I couldn't get my then 5 and 6 year-old off it. They talked about it for weeks! Hmm, maybe it's sad that this is our largest excitement? Nope, totally worth the hype.

Bathroom unpleasantries are mostly left to chubby bears in a toilet paper commercial, but I feel the importance of the matter requires us to get uncomfortable for a moment. Especially after the great toilet paper shortage of 2020.

Let's start with the obvious, wiping with toilet paper has been sold to the public as the hygienic way to clean up. It's not. <u>Dr. Evan Golstein</u> is a rectal surgeon in New York City and believes bidets are ideal:

"Charmin and all these brands have done a great job making us think that toilet paper is hygienic. It's not."

Take a second and think about what toilet paper does with the action of wiping. Wiping smears poop around, it doesn't really clean it. Wiping transplants fecal matter in other areas. Oh, you're not eating and reading are you? You may want to step away from the food because it gets worse. Let's talk about anal tearing.

The good doctor indicated wiping can lead to injury. Toilet paper is abrasive and an aggresive wipe or finger break-thrugh can lead to anal tearing. The skin around your anus is delicate and thin which makes it susceptible to cuts. Cuts lead to bleeding and pain.

Research on other benefits of bidets are still outstanding. As it stands, research that has been completed weighs-in on both sides of the fence. The majority believe bidets are ideal for people with arthritis, frequent hemorrhoids, fissures, and itchy anus. I didn't know that last one was a thing either; it sounds horrific. But, the words that really get me here from wiping are *fecal residue*. Ew.

Another general caution is that women should not use the bidet for...extracurricular activities. Using a bidet too much can change the normal bacteria you are supposed to have down under. Safe bidet rules are in usage amount, water pressure, and water temperature.

Frankly, I am surprised bidets are not <u>standard</u> in American homes. They have been around for over 300 years (centuries in some older cultures) and are standard in most other countries. Bidets are environmentally friendly and easy on the pocket book by both lowered utility usage and zero toilet paper purchases.

It's possible America didn't warm up to bidets during the Industrial Revolution because soldiers were first introduced to bidets in overseas brothels during World War II. It's not cricket to tell the wife "I really like the one they had at the brothel, it was so sanitary." It was a stigma that stuck: Bidets are for sex workers.

Since sustainability is trending at the moment, it may be time to reintroduce the bidet to America. Here come the fun facts. Bidets use ⅛ of a gallon of water vs. 37 gallons of water used to make a roll of toilet paper. America uses 34 million rolls of toilet paper a day. The 384 trees you saved by purchasing a bidet thank you. That is how many trees it takes to make the toilet paper you will use in a lifetime.

Bidet advocates stand firm in the belief that bidets help with fewer rashes, urinary tract infections, hemorrhoids, and other medical issues. Most bidets come with a blow-dryer feature so you don't have to deal with any gross, stank issues. Bidets deserve a shout out. What doesn't deserve a shout out is bathroom noise. No one wants to hear that.

Soundproof Your Bathroom

Bathrooms are the keepers of the proverbial throne wrapped in porcelain, marble, and tile. This combination is brimming with acoustic possibilities. Sound bounces off the sleek cold surroundings with wild ferocity breaking through the sound barrier of doors and walls.

Jimmy Kimmel capitalized on this fact by inviting musical guests to perform remotely from their bathrooms. These performances captured the true natural acoustics and amplified the musicians talents. It was sobering.

Not all talent needs amplification and recognition. Unless your butthole can belch out a symphony akin to PhilHarmonic, I shouldn't have to hear it. Family is destined to share everything, however, private moments in the bathroom are intimate and sacred. Bathrooms are for the evacuation of all evil things which includes:

- Clearing your mind
- Finding a second of peace in chaos; and
- A safe space to mentally check-in with yourself before spewing words you can't take back, word vomit is real

The bathroom is nature's diary of mental and physical release. It is a blessing and courtesy that this room is soundproof for you and your family's protection. There are several ways to soundproof a bathroom without remodeling. Adding mass to the room helps. By mass, I mean fluffy towels in a rack, or more pictures. FYI, I don't buy into any of that (I watched Jimmy Kimmel).

If you are remodeling your bathroom, do your family a solid and add insulation to the walls, floor, and ceiling. Rock wool is designed for soundproofing if you are going that route. You can also install acoustic underlay to any subflooring and acoustic tiles to the ceiling. Soundproofing a bathroom is largely a DIY thing, but hiring professionals isn't all that expensive and well worth the money.

According to <u>Home Advisor</u> the typical cost to soundproof one room is $380 to $590; and that is an average sized room, not a small bathroom. This price does not include the removal of existing material. You would pay this amount for a few months of rugs which aren't as adept at securing absorption of sound.

But, really, how much is too much when you are talking about bathroom courtesy? Some things you can't put a price on.

CHAPTER 7

Legendary Stories & Sexy Fireplaces

Storytelling and fires go together like marshmallows, chocolate, and graham crackers. Fires are hypnotizing and serve as an excellent TV alternative for a night. No one knows how fire came to be. Some think lightning struck a tree and one man saw it, ran to get his buddies, and they huddled around it discussing caveman quantum physics while accidentally discovering how to keep the fire burning. That sounds about right. Some think fire was no accident at all, and still others think fire was from divine intervention or mythical heroes.

In Hindu mythology, the god of fire, Agni, represents the essential energy of life in the universe. He created the sun and stars and consumes bad things so other things can live. Agni can make you immortal and purify dead souls of their sins. Cremation makes a bundle of sense with this belief.

Chinese mythology has the grand stories of Hui Lu, the magician and fire god. He would set his 100 firebirds loose to start fires across the country. He wasn't the only god with fire. There was a hierarchy. Lo Hsuan was at the top with his red cloak, hair, and beard. All it took was a princess to quench his flames with her mist and dew cloak.

Greek mythology had Prometheus as the bringer of fire. Stealing it from the gods and giving it to man.

Native Americans credit an evil spirit for hiding fire that a coyote found and stole for the people. In other versions of the story, it is a wolf or woodpecker. I like the coyote version. He cleverly tricks two monsters guarding the flames.

African stories result in animals giving fire to humans. One such story is an Ostrich who guarded fire under its wing and a praying mantis stole it, which destroyed the mantis. However, the ashes of that destruction yielded two mantises.

In Brazil, Indians of the Amazon River basin claim a jaguar saved a boy and offered refuge in its cave. The jaguar cooked over a fire and the boy stole a hot coal and took it to his people so they could cook.

These stories are very different, but one thing ties them all together. These legendary stories have been told around campfires since ancient times. The first campfire stories are about 400,000 years old.

Anthropologists at the University of Utah conducted a <u>study</u> in the 1970s about the Ju Hoan tribe's day and night conversations. The tribe lived mainly as hunters and gatherers at the time. The researchers found that daytime talk was focused on economics, land rights, complaints, and the day-to-day running of civilization. But when the sun slept and the fire extended the night, 81% of firelight conversation was devoted to telling fantastic stories. Thus, solidifying their social network.

"Stories told by firelight put listeners on the same emotional wavelength and elicited understanding, trust, and sympathy." Wiessner adds that fire still serves that purpose today: "The power of the flame is reproduced in our homes through fireplaces and candles."

We still love a good story and a roaring fireplace to cozy up to. There are three movies that have ruined me when it comes to fireplaces. No other fireplace in any home has swept me off my feet. These regal, mammoth hearths are the gold standard in which I judge every fireplace against and nothing has weighed in to their equivalent.

#1   The Haunting - This fireplace is the perfect candy cane swirl of innocence and sinister. For example see: https://co.pinterest.com/pin/505388389412077678/

#2   Citizen Kane - The wide open stage as a fire roars behind you is the closest to feeling what Hansel and Gretel felt. For example see: https://www.pinterest.com/pin/296182112977357059/

#3   Harry Potter - You never knew where you were going to end up - every fireplace held an adventure. For example see: https://iamapotterhead.weebly.com/transportation.html

Some scientists believe the ability to make fire is what separates us from the animals and not the opposable thumb. Fire is a fierce force of nature and critical to human survival. If you doubt that, watch any episode of Survivor. I get most of what I know from the TV.

In ancient cultures, fire was sacred and sometimes worshipped. Fire was used in nearly every ritual in every known culture. It changed the very way ancient cultures lived. As our knowledge of fire evolved, it remained a necessity in heating homes, cooking food, and keeping beasts away so you could sleep while camping. Fire was bigger than the internet and acted as the centerpiece of home life and socialization.

The <u>move</u> of fire from outdoor pits to indoor vaults was quick. Early homes, like 500 BC, had a fire pit in the center of the home. The home was literally built around the fire with a hole in the roof for smoke to escape.

Those bloody Roman bakers upped the ante by inventing fireplaces with a flue which funneled smoke through pipes. The fire was still located in the center of the room. It wasn't until 1066 AD that fire pits in the center of the room moved to the wall with a new contraption called the chimney. The fireplace may have moved, but the gathering around it, the nucleus of all things social, remained the same.

In the 1600s <u>through</u> the early 1700s, fireplaces were monstrously wide, deep, and open - like my movie favorites. You were able to walk into them and maneuver around easily with plenty of elbow room. Some fireplaces were more wide than tall, either way, they were beautiful beasts holding the heart of an active home.

Some homes had multiple fires in several rooms working on a central chimney and flue network so the entire home could be heated at once. The network of fireplaces was designed to hold heat in the home during the winter. Most of these fireplaces didn't have mantels, not until the 1800s - that's when they got bedazzled.

The 1800s fireplace was dressed in decorative paneling, surrounded by intricate mantels, dressings, and home pieces of every size and shape. Fireplaces were an item of grandeur. Then some pompous, American-born, British physicist mucked things up.

Sir Benjamin Thompson, Count Rumford, FRS (more initials after his name than 4 doctors) decided he wanted to create a revolution in thermodynamics and created the firebox that we know today. Yeah, sure, it radiates more heat into the room with better exhausts to prevent backdrafts; but I like my inefficient, massive stoneworks. It was not meant to be mon cheri.

By the Industrial Revolution, homes were urbanized and burning coal not wood. Fireplaces were smaller, decorative, and still useful but robbed of their grandiose size and castle-esque beauty. Fireplaces were further innovated in 1990 with the central heat wood-burning fireplace and the 1995 electric fireplace.

Fireplaces were still seen as the family gathering place and an immortal shrine of comfort and grace. Fireplaces continue to be a highly-desired element in homes today. Amusingly, so is the backyard firepit. Legendary stories have been told around fireplaces for thousands of years and will continue to be told for a thousand more. Wow, kind of went all Twilight there. Fireplaces crackle with romance and it is hard not to get lost in their charm.

Sitting around a fire and <u>watching</u> it DOES lower your blood pressure, who knew? Scientists believe our soothing feelings when watching a fire stem from the fire gatherings held in prehistoric times. The love of fire is innate. The University of Alabama asked 226 people to watch a fireplace on TV. Blood pressure was taken before and after the viewing. One group watched a fire with sound and the longer they watched, the more relaxed they were. Another group watched an upside down fire with no sound and their blood pressure increased.

Researchers believe that when we watch fire, we are completely immersed in the blaze, like being hypnotized. The fire consumes our focus, calms us, and reduces anxiety. Fires were the center of everything in prehistoric times and the most enjoyable events were fire socials. The social part of fire explains why research participants that exhibited prosocial behavior, like empathy and altruism, scored higher in total relaxation.

Fireplace Is Life

What does all of this tell us? Fireplaces should be a requirement in every home. Although desired for their looks, they need to be designed to heat the house or converted to wood-burning stoves. The fact is, this world has had a few close calls of an apocalypse and even more coming down the pike. Investment in getting a fireplace that works may not only be trending, it may save your life. Fireplaces may take a violent shove from amenity to necessity. At a minimum, fireplaces add value to the home.

You could also co-sign on the fact that natural gas fireplaces are a source of sustainable, <u>efficient</u> heat lowering utility bills. Most families spend time in the family room or kitchen which are usually close together so zone heating becomes a viable option and you can turn down the thermostat.

Central heating units supply heat to the whole house and cost about $1.12 to $1.49 running one hour at 75,000 to 100,000 Btu. Natural gas fireplaces run at about 30,000 Btu and cost $0.45 and heat the zones you are spending your time in. Gas rises, so it's a bonus if your living rooms are downstairs. There are a few things to look for if you decide on a natural gas fireplace:

- AFUE = Annual Fuel Utilization Efficiency rating
- Direct vent gas fireplaces burn efficiently
- Intermittent pilot ignite (IPI) means it lites the pilot light when you need it rather than always have it lit - reducing half the gas used by the fireplace

Gas fireplaces are easier to <u>install</u> than their wood burning counterparts. The average cost including installation is between $2,650 to $5,800 depending on the model you select and the location of installation. They pay for themselves.

Nothing can compare to the hearth lifestyle a fireplace provides for your home. Looking for the perfect fireplace is like looking for the perfect home, there is always a story to go with it.

The Wild Ones

Some homes are so beautiful, and redonkulous, that the upkeep would sink the pocket book of a normal person. There are many homes that started off with the best of intentions but some misfortune crumbled the dream causing the dream and home to be abandoned or have a stunning legacy. It's a coin toss. Here are just a few.

Carlton Island, Cape Vincent, New York $495k

https://www.realtor.com/news/unique-homes/carleton-island-abandoned-villa/

William Wyckoff was the inventor of the typewriter. You can imagine the windfall that came his way with the discovery. He used his fortune to build this grand mansion next to the water as a vacation home. The scene was picturesque, calming, sublime perfection. Unfortunately, his wife died a month before the home was ready and he suffered a heart attack and died on the FIRST night of occupancy. Although the home passed to his sons, the family fortune was lost during the Great Depression.

General Electric owned the home briefly in the 1930s and was going to use it for a company retreat but World War II diverted their efforts. At that time, contractors were granted permission to remove windows, doors, and any other items necessary for the war effort. This left the home exposed to the elements. General Electric also tore down the tower as a safety hazard and enclosed the home with barbed-wire to prevent hazards befalling curious teens.

The home has been vacant since 1927 bouncing on and off the market. It will take millions of dollars to restore the home to its former glory in its prime location. The current owners are aware of the expense and prefer to live in a nearby cottage.

Thousands of potential investors have inquired about the property, but the estimate to repair it came to $10 to 12 million. The biggest challenge is there are no utilities connected to the home and the island is only accessible by boat. This means a barge would have to float materials which increases the restoration cost by 30%.

Should any investor swallow the reparation costs, it would be an ideal location with exquisite accommodations as a weekend getaway. The home boasts 15,000 square feet, 11 bedrooms, and nearly 7 acres with three waterfronts complete with tour boats frequently passing by full of New Yorkers and Canadians.

Elkins Park, Philadelphia, Pennsylvania $16.5 million

https://www.mansionglobal.com/articles/philadelphia-s-110-room-lynnewood-hall-gets-1-million-price-cut-75322

This is a colossal beast of a home with an equally enormous amount of history. I will give you the condensed version. PAB Widener was the most prolific collector of fine art. He acquired his fortune by supplying meat to the Union Army during the Civil War. Being an intelligent, innovative man, he invested his fortune into becoming a founding partner of the Philadelphia Traction Company. The Company built public transport systems in Philadelphia, New York, and Chicago.

The venture allowed him to further his domination in wealth and prosperity to become a principal partner in US Steel, American Tobacco Company, and Standard Oil. Dayum, dude is a baller. His vision and conquests made him one of the 100 richest Americans--ever. He was dubbed a 'robber baron' (ruthless and unscrupulous business practices) and a philanthropist. His holdings allowed him to purchase Linwood Hall in the 1880s as a summer vacation home and continued to build, alter, and enhance the structure and property for several years.

In 1896 when his wife died, he gave their townhouse in Philadelphia to the Free Library and moved into Linwood as his main home. He set architects upon the palace and changed the name to Lynnewood Hall. The project took 2 years and $8 million to complete the 70,000 square foot neo-classical masterpiece. The home swells with 110 rooms. A staff was required, a big one, over 35 employed domestic staff and 60 upkeep staff for the surrounding 480 acres. The ground floor of the east-west section contains a 2,250 square foot ballroom that comfortably accommodates

1,000 guests. Classy. I won't even speak about the walnut and gold-leaf pilaster with oval murals in the ceiling - sheesh. But, we were talking about misfortune earlier - here it comes.

All of the Widener's lived at the mansion within their respective grand apartments. In 1912, George and his son Harry were on the Titanic returning for a grand wedding that was to take place in the ballroom. This was the beginning of the end. In 1915, there was one surviving child left, Joseph. Joseph inherited the estate and $60 million.

Joseph ended up selling and donating about 2,000 pieces of art that were in his father's collection and valued at $18.5 million to the National Gallery in Washington. In 1943 when Joseph died, his heirs sold off the remaining contents at Lynnwood in an auction raising $337,000. Neither his children, nor his grandchildren wanted the responsibility (or cost) of the huge mansion and it stood empty except for a caretaker to watch over the grounds. A caretaker, one.

The family sold 220 acres to a developer who built community housing and in 1948, the same developer bought the mansion and its 36 acres of landscaped gardens at a sheriff's auction for $130,000. A controversial preacher named Dr. Carl McIntire paid $192,000 for the enormous mansion and converted it to a seminary where he proceeded to strip the house and gardens of its Greber fountain, walnut panelling, marble fireplaces and balustrades to fund his mission.

Dr. McIntire failed to pay the mortgage and in 2006, the bank foreclosed. The house sat empty and unprotected. It is eligible to be added to the National Register of Historic Places, but it has not been. The current owner, Richard Yoon of the First Korean Church has it on the market. If I could buy it, I would. The Gilded Age magnificence includes a swimming pool, wine cellars, a farm, and an electrical power plant. I was sold when I saw the entryway.

However, just redoing the exterior will run you about $10 million. To restore the inside, the price is closer to $50 <u>million</u>. The home is in danger of being demolished and beyond repair. If neglect continues, the home will be gone within the next 5 to 10 years.

Yo! Amazon! Are you looking for an office site on the east coast?? This is the question being asked by the current realtor. He also added the buyer can get state tax credits for restoring the site.

Arlington, Natchez, Mississippi

https://www.loveproperty.com/gallerylist/92978/tour-arlington-the-mysterious-abandoned-mansion-in-natchez-mississippi

This Federal mansion and historical landmark is crumbling into ruin despite the rich history. The 55 acres surrounding the home has been untended for several years. No one knows exactly when it was built but we do know that the local sheriff, Lewis Evans, had acquired the land in the early 1800s and sold it to Jonathan Thompson, a real estate speculator in 1814. When the home was nominated for the National Register of Historic Places, it suggests John White designed the home for his wife, Jane Surget White between 1816 and 1819.

The picture above shows the regal home in 1934. Unfortunately, it is a sight that John White would never get to see. In 1819, right when the home was completed, John White died in a yellow fever epidemic. After Jane's death in 1825, her sister, Mrs. Binaman inherited the property and the deed rested with the family until bought in the 19th century by Mississippi Supreme Court Judge, Samuel Stillman Boyd.

Judge Boyd passed in 1867 and the property was vacant until 1917 when Mrs. Gilette purchased it and lived happily there until 1924. The treasures from every previous owner had remained in the mansion to be enjoyed and passed from owner to owner. Eventually, the property was sold to Hubert Barnum and presented to his wife, Annie, as a wedding gift. She loved it so much that she remained at Arlington (the home) even though she owned the Monmouth mansion in the city.

She cared for the home and added treasurers of her own, including prized first edition books. Misfortune struck when Mrs. Barnum's one-year-old grandchild died in a tragic accident at the property. Mrs. Barnum passed in 1960 leaving the property to her daughter, Anne Gwin Vaughan. The family moved into Arlington and cared for it for several decades. In 1991, both Anne and her husband passed away, leaving it to their son, Dr. Thomas Vaughan who owns it to this day.

Dr. Vaughan lives in Jackson and did not move into the property. He left the mansion to deteriorate after his parents' deaths. In September 2002, fire engulfed Arlington. Many of the home's antiques and other treasurers were salvaged and restored, but the home remained a shell.

Since Dr. Vaughan did not maintain adequate insurance, the Natchez Preservation Commission sued him for demolition by neglect. In 2009, Dr. Vaughan was found guilty and ordered to pay a $259 fine much to the disappointment of the Commission. The Commission was hoping to overhaul the mansion and recoup the fees through fines to the good doctor. The doctor didn't even show up to court.

In 2012, officials brought Dr. Vaughan to task again for creating a dangerous situation with vandals, vagrants, and the property not being kept to code. In 2013, he pleaded guilty to the overgrown lot. In 2014, he looked into selling the property under a judge's supervision. He has since changed his mind and the property sits and waits.

Rockwell House, Milledgeville, Georgia

https://www.loveproperty.com/gallerylist/92978/tour-arlington-the-mysterious-abandoned-mansion-in-natchez-mississippi

Rockwell was built for Colonel Samuel Rockwell, an attorney and slaveholder. The history is intriguing and includes stories of gold buried here - somewhere. Colonel Rockwell died in 1841 and the property continued to flow from owner to owner through the open arms of Midgeville's high society crowd. It was Dr. Robert Watson who purchased the property in 1962. Would you believe there is another story of misfortune? There seems to be a theme.

In 1969, Dr. Watson had big plans for the property and hired workers to renovate the upstairs. Unfortunately, the workers were attempting to remove paint with a blowtorch and set the place ablaze. The damage was extensive and Dr. Watson vacated the premises. Fortunately, Rockwell has been purchased by investors who are restoring the property to its former glory.

Elda Castle, Ossining, New York

https://www.loveproperty.com/gallerylist/92978/tour-arlington-the-mysterious-abandoned-mansion-in-natchez-mississippi

This castle sticks out among the 50 acres of woodland, doesn't it? The abandoned stone mansion was built and designed by David Thomas Abercrombie - yes, Abercrombie and Fitch - and his wife, Lucy Abbot Cate.

This castle even has a clever name, made with the first letter of each of the couple's children in the order they were born. The 1920s castle is 4,337 square feet and looks like something out of a fairy tail. Abercrombie died shortly after the completion of the fairy tale. Renovating a house is enough to put you in your grave, especially a 25-room elegant beast. Through the years, several owners have attempted to restore the castle but none have been successful. The current price is set at $3.2 million and is waiting for its prince on the real estate market.

Mongo's Castle, Memphis, Tennessee

https://www.loveproperty.com/gallerylist/92978/tour-arlington-the-mysterious-abandoned-mansion-in-natchez-mississippi

This 1896 beauty is the creation of Robert Brinkey Snowden who anointed the home Ashlar Hall due to all the Ashlar stone used in the structure. This is 11,000 square feet of fabulous. In 1983, the home was placed on the National Register of Historic Places and in the 90s became Mongo's Castle after the zany new owner, Robert Hodges.

Hodges appointed himself the Prince of Mongo and transformed the stone fortress into a nightclub. He also says he is a 333-year-old alien from planet Zambodia. Got to love this guy. The club was packed for years, maybe a bit too packed. The authorities shut it down for overcrowding. No problem for an interstellar dude. He shipped in 800 pounds of sand and transformed the car park outside into a beach. It didn't go over nearly as well as he thought. The Prince abandoned the property, probably returning to Zambodia. Juan Montoya purchased it in 2017 and plans to renovate it, much to the delight of earthlings everywhere.

Dundas Castle, Roscoe, New York

https://www.loveproperty.com/gallerylist/92978/tour-arlington-the-mysterious-abandoned-mansion-in-natchez-mississippi

This robust neo-Gothic treasure sits in a green sea of 1,000 acres in the Catskill Mountains. The solemn dwelling has been nicknamed the Castle of Sorrow.

Ralph Wurts-Dundas commissioned the castle in the late 1910s. The commission was on such a grandiose scale that he sadly died in 1921 before its scheduled completion. His widow, Josephine was committed to the asylum shortly after his death and the property passed to their daughter, Muriel. You see the theme too now, right?

Muriel's parents had left a fortune of $40 million; however, Muriel never saw it. The bulk of the inheritance had been squandered by the castle caretakers. This left no money to continue the endeavor and construction ceased in 1924. Muriel moved overseas and ended up in the psychiatric hospital, following in her mother's footsteps.

Upon her death in 1949, the castle was purchased by a group of freemasons. It remained a retreat until the 1970s and has been vacant ever since. Ghost stories surround the castle in which Josephine lurks around the grounds and the water in the estate's ponds turn to blood during a full moon. Now that's a party.

Dicksonia Plantation, Lowndesboro, Alabama

https://www.loveproperty.com/gallerylist/92978/tour-arlington-the-mysterious-abandoned-mansion-in-natchez-mississippi

The ruins of this 1830 plantation was remodeled in Greek Revival style during the 1850s and has many stories to tell.

The home ran the circle of prominent Southern family ownership and settled on Robert Dickson in 1901 who promptly named it Dicksonia. Dicksonia was promptly obliterated by fire in 1939 and a replica was built on the ashes the following year. Fire found the replica just as tasty as the original. Fire consumed the replica in 1964. The Dickson family found the home irreparable and abandoned it to the care of mother nature. In the 1990s, a new owner purchased the scorched mansion and preserved what remained rather than rebuilding. He has been rewarded with the home featured in movies, fashion shoots and you can even get married on the grounds.

Mystery mansion, New York

https://www.loveproperty.com/gallerylist/92978/tour-arlington-the-mysterious-abandoned-mansion-in-natchez-mississippi

This 57-room mansion was built in the 1930s. The owner was a whacko known to buy huge estates and then bail, leaving them to rot with several belongings inside. Keeping true to form, the owner left this one in 1976. The mansion was abandoned with furnishings inside including pianos and crystal chandeliers. Vintage toys were strewn around the house elevating the creepiness. Surprisingly, the home is in decent shape despite the horror vibe. Speaking of horror, let's talk basements.

CHAPTER 8

Basements Aren't Just For Bodies Anymore

Ah, the basement. In my childhood, the basement was my dad's temple. As you descended the precarious stairs, bands like KISS and Zeppelin reverberated sharply off the cool cement wall sounding board. Scantily clad posters of women, the caliber of Farrah Faucet, Marilyn Monroe, and various bombshell pinups straddling motorcycles haphazardly hung with tape on the walls.

The grand centerpiece was a colossal foosball table, usually with me lurking underneath to eavesdrop on my dad and his friends in their smoke-hazed, caveman talks. On occasion, I was welcomed into the group (daddy's girl) to recite my worldly answers' to life's complex questions of the week, much to the amusement of all. I was provided with an olive-colored bean bag serving as my throne of inclusivity. There was always a distinct pungent aroma, and it confused me because there was nothing cooking--I didn't identify the aroma till much later in life.

When I was a teenager, the basement temple torch was passed to me. The cement walls were replaced by elegant plywood dually separating and creating a bedroom, living room, and bathroom in a maze that shamed office cubicles. The posters of bombshells were replaced with Angus Young (AC/DC), Lars Ulrich (Metallica), Nirvana, Joan Jett, angry girl bands, and boy bands I'm too embarrassed to commit to in writing. There was no foosball table (sold to refurbish the basement), and the weed-aroma had been vanquished some time ago by my mother who had promptly chased it out of the house upon discovery--with dad's friends.

Basements are a nostalgic place for me and will always hold a special place in my heart with fond memories. It is where my girlfriends and I contemplated life and schemed misbehavior--struggling in that awkward area between childhood and adulthood. I scribbled stories, poetry, and songs in journals for hours at a time and dreamed of the day I would be a famous artist (singer or writer) and flee the small town--how Taylor Swift of me, right?

So, imagine my surprise when some news station announced the findings of a survey and stated: "When people think basements, most Americans carry a sense of fear and reserve the abandoned square footage for storage."

Wait, what? Clearly there is some mistake. I ambitiously started digging through history to discover why people are scared of my sentimental, coming of age utopia. Was it Romans or Hippies? If you read the prior Tour of Insanity book, you know my love/hate relationship with both.

Roman Home Architecture & Cityscapes

Romans are credited for a lot of architectural wonders. Cities were large, crowded, metropolises with public works--but at the same time, extremely cramped in an effort for everyone to have access to facilities. Personal space never seemed to be an issue with Romans.

Most Romans lived in multi-story (like 5 or 6 story) apartments balanced on a main floor composed of storefronts and shops. The lower floors would house the wealthy shop owners and the hierarchical totem pole would rise up to the least wealthy. This jenga pile organization had to do with the first floor being the only floor with running water and heat from the basement.

When I say basement, I don't really mean basement like we know them. Romans used a hypocaust to heat the main floors of apartments, kingly townhomes, and stunning upper crust villas. Homes were either heated by charcoal burning in a bronze tin, or placing a fire in a make-shit underground lair to heat the air so it rises--the hypocaust.

Townhomes would have no windows on the first floor to ensure dust and noise from the busy street stayed outside and the home, and private bath, stayed toasty warm. For fresh air, townhomes were equipped with a central open-air atrium. The apartment upper structures were not afforded this luxury and most were prone to fires. Because fires were common, kitchens were not allowed in the apartments and meals were commonly purchased from local bars and vendors--much like a food court.

The first floor of the apartment walls were made of clay and brick while upper levels were made of wood. Fire would bypass the downstairs and engulf the upper floors in flames before occupants could escape the crowded, unsanitary conditions.

After the great fire of 64 A.D. leveled a large portion of city housing, Romans adopted the practice of using concrete mixed with stone. They also built new structures on top of old structures by filling in the buildings below with dirt which transformed what was a roof into a solid foundation. This practice makes the three-millenia underbelly of modern Rome one of the most intriguing layer-cakes of archaeological sites in the world. But back to the point, were there basements? In my humble opinion, hypocausts don't count.

What you are looking at is one of many original streets below Rome's hustle and bustle of daily life. The deep cavity's structures confined within are filled with earth supporting the buildings above. The entombed street was hollowed out so we could view the epic echoes of Roman footsteps. In other areas, underground structures have been cleared of dirt and welcome tourists. Most entries to the underground Rome are via churches.

Ah, now we are onto something. Christianity was practiced in privacy among friends and family, guess where. Basements. Emperor Constantine pioneered the building of churches in Rome, but before that, religion was a hushed, secret affair. The street above is one such entryway. The Basilica di San Clemente dates back to the 8th century, however, the sub-basement is part of a well-preserved mansion dating back to the 4th century.

The mansion was a perfect location for a Roman overseeing the operations of the Colosseum. Some evidence suggests this could have been the structure housing Rome's mint (Fort Knox). In the mansion beneath the earth is a shrine to the Persian god Mithras that was worshipped primarily by Roman soldiers and government officials.

The Colosseum is a majestic structure to behold and the shows weren't half-bad either. The pyrotechnics rivaled Vegas Strip shows. The Colosseum had a maze of passageways in a subterranean level which housed the special-effects machinery, wild animals, and gladiators. The passageways are an overachieving, sophisticated web of connections to several surrounding buildings including the gladiator training schools (ludi).

Don't give the Roman's too much credit just yet. When I started researching basements, I looked under wine cellars. Where you find Roman's, you find wine, right? Roman's didn't store wine in cellars, at first. Wine storage was on the main floor in a cella vinaria or fumantoriries. The Romans would fill the room with smoke to strangle oxygen for preservation, but the warm room would accelerate spoilage. We explore wine cellars in the next chapter.

I cannot say for certain that Romans created the basement, but I'm in the habit of placing blame on them, so it fits. The Colosseum is a large-scale functioning commercial basement which is a bit different from the basements we know today.

What About Root Cellars

Ancient civilizations, like prehistoric ancient civilizations, buried their food. Some root cellars are still standing today while the homes that utilized them are no more. Most root cellars were separate from the main dwelling because they were mostly created from already existing natural landscapes.

Europeans brought the practice of using root cellars when they colonized America. Root cellars were the first refrigerators and were of profound importance to survival, especially during harsh winters. The dark, cool environment root cellars afforded prevented meat and produce from spoiling because they were about 40 degrees cooler than the outside temperature. For example see: https://www.loc.gov/resource/hhh.mn0482.photos/?sp=2

During the Great Depression and WWII, the government implored Americans to use their root cellars and build more of them. This is why you see them sprinkled across the American landscape. But, does a refrigerator make for a basement? Root cellars had the specific purpose of food storage and are fairly creepy with spider webs, insects, and a damp wafty smell in every corner that makes you shiver considering what could be causing it. Speaking of smells, maybe I know why people are scared of basements.

A Killer's Guide To Basements

Serial killers and sexual predators have a nasty habit of leaving bodies lying about in basements and, upon discovery, terrorize people and soil a basement's good name. The privacy and natural sound barrier the underground space provides is ideal for predators to act on their urges in a controlled environment. It also serves as a great place to hide the deeds--at least for a while.

One of the most dedicated, meticulous basement enthusiasts was H.H. Holmes. The Holmes castle was built specifically for the purpose of murder. It is believed he killed up to 200 people from 1891 to 1894 but only confessed to 27. The castle is in Chicago and the good doctor used it to trap, psychologically torture, and kill his victims.

To conceal his plans, he hired and fired builders after adding specific renovations such as pipes to pump gas into bedrooms, a room geared to suffocate people, and the piece de la resistance--the basement used for murder and experimentation. He was hanged in Philadelphia in 1896. What happened to the castle? Arsen by unknown assailants. A post office covers the sleeping bones of the structure. For picture see: https://hollycarden.com/blog/2016/1/11/making-the-h-h-holmes-murder-castle

Holmes is speculated to be Jack the Ripper. He was in England when the murders occurred and the intent of the murders Holmes committed was never for financial gain--just like Ripper. Witness descriptions also matched Holmes. Both removed the organs of the victims, something a doctor could do.

The world may never know, although his grandson believes the two are the same. What we can say is Holmes was an innovative architect, and brings the malicious perspective of basements into view. Basements are largely designed for a specific purpose. Good, evil, or otherwise.

Foundations: Going Down Under

Once we know the purpose of our basement, holding gladiators or hiding indiscretions, it is the foundation that makes the dream a reality and drives the design. Foundations act as the support for everything built above it. They also prevent the structure sinking into the ground under its own weight.

Foundations are carefully placed and assessed to buffer strength, otherwise you end up with the leaning Tower of Pisa. Ideally the weight of the structure rests on the foundation, not in the soft earth. Where you live and the era you live in dictates what type of foundation and basement you have, if any. In foundations, geographic location is EVERYTHING. In Nevada, the soil is completely different than in Pennsylvania.

Foundations go back 12,000 years. For example, neolithic Switzerland built homes on foundations made of wooden piles driven into shallow lakes in gigantic moat-like fashion as protection from dangerous predators. This was early post-in-ground construction. Babylonians used reed mats to erect colossal monuments and Egyptians' magnificent pyramids relied on stone blocks resting on the bedrock. Both forms are early padstones.

Romans, those little scoundrels, created cement. The use of cement in foundation engineering propelled them leaps and bounds ahead of their comrades. Engineers created structurally sound rules and regulations for buildings and their foundations. This explains the pyrotechnics and gladiator holding cells at the Colosseum and neighboring civic and social-use commercial buildings.

The strength of a foundation in most cases depends on how deep you can dig. The shallower a foundation is, the less strength it has. It's just like pitching a tent on a windy day. You want the stakes deep to prevent it from becoming airborne. During the mid-20th century, builders could dig more than 100 feet in the ground. This was deep enough for metal pylons to create enormous skyscrapers. Malaysia's Petronas Towers built in 1966 hold the record for deepest foundation--374 feet underground.

In a chicken vs. egg scenario, it was the Roman ingenuity in formulating cement coupled with the innovative tools to dig deep that produced a bonafide basement. Basements, at first, were primarily used to house the mechanics of the house like a boiler, or provide access to the mechanics like a crawlspace. Or, to hide people, bootleg, or smuggle other goods. Basements before 1948 largely grew out of cellars and to draw a line in the sand, we will say that basements dug before 1948 have been remodeled or should have been by now. Why is 1948 the jumping point?

Backhoe loaders were invented in 1948, just in time for the suburban homes being built in the 1950s to feature fully finished basements. Finished basements prior to this were a sign of wealth in larger estate homes. Finished basements would include a separate service entrance and living quarters for maids, gardeners, cooks, nannies, and house staff.

Innovations in dealing with basement moisture such as sump pumps (1946) and dehumidifiers (1902) became less commercial and more residential in affordability and availability. The burst of energy during the industrial revolution reshaped homes all over America, including basements. This is a before & after basement remodel from the late 1940s. For picture see: https://clickamericana. com/topics/home-garden/vintage-basement-decor-from-40s-50s-see-25-creative-remodels

Remodels of basements in older homes influenced homebuilders of the 1950s into selling a more themed approach to basement living. Along with the preinstalled front and back yards, homeowner association rules on mowing and maintenance, white-picket fences, and prefab communities; basements fit right into the American Dream. Here are a few ads from the 1950s-- the birth of the basement havens:

https://clickamericana.com/topics/home-garden/vintage-basement-decor-from-40s-50s-see-25-creative-remodels

These vintage basements doubled the living space of a home. In 1950s America, you could afford more space, effectively bringing more value to your dollar. Plus, with the cold war raging (1947-1991), the public was encouraged to bunker down--a great selling point. Some, even made their basements into fallout shelters (#prepperlife).

Basement Bunkers

In 1999, the movie Blast From The Past was released. Brendan Fraser plays Adam Webber, who was born in a fallout shelter. The movie takes place during the Cuban Missile Crisis. Adam's mom was scurried into a fallout shelter while pregnant after a plane crashes near the Webber home. Calvin, the overzealous, eccentric father, had believed the deafening noise to be atomic warfare. Adam reaches adulthood frozen in time with all that is 1960ish.

When the family runs low on supplies, Adam must return to the surface to forage, and at the pleading of his mom--look for a wife to bring back. In doing so, he finds out they were never under attack. It's a cute story and during the 1950s-60s, was completely relevant with the threat of Soviet nuclear attacks as tensions escalated.

Community shelters were constructed beneath municipal buildings. Government bunkers were carved into hillsides and families across the country created fallouts either from basements or as separate dwellings. People falsely believed these shelters would protect them from nuclear catastrophe. For example see: https://onmilwaukee.com/articles/fallout-shelter-spelunking

In 1955, the Eisenhower administration and Federal Civil Defense Administration (FCDA) urged Americans to keep seven days of food and water on hand at a minimum. If only we would have had this kind of warning about toilet paper during COVID. The FCDA even released a Grandma's Pantry initiative supplying fallout friendly food. Ofcourse, popular brands jumped on that bandwagon.

The US Department of Agriculture developed Doomsday food and distributed it in early 1960. The brainchild of that venture was the All-Purpose Survival Cracker. The shelf life is 3,000 years. How do they know the shelflife is 3,000 years?, you might ask. Because they have been consumed for thousands of years by Babylonians, Chinese emperors, and scientists found and ate some from an Egyptian pyramid.

The cracker must have been good because the Pentagon enlisted Sunshine Biscuits, Kroger, Southern Biscuit Company, Nabisco, and Keebler to make them. By 1964, 20 billion survival crackers had been distributed.

In mid-1961, John F. Kennedy reinforced American prepping beliefs by expanding the nation's civil defense programs. He swiftly called for more than $200 million budget appropriations to construct fallout shelters. JFK aggressively urged Americans to build private shelters. During the time, there were about 60,000 in 1961 which skyrocketed to 200,000 by 1965.

The Office of Civil Defense promoted home shelters and published manuals and videos for American Doomsday DIY. The cost, roughly $150-200 for the bare minimum. Underground fallouts were constructed and rooted deep all over the country. It didn't help much that Russia had missiles 90 miles from the US in Cuba and <u>warned</u> the West with the following quote:

"It would take really very few multi-megaton nuclear bombs to wipe out your small and densely populated countries and kill you instantly in your lairs."

It is probably this one sentence spoken in a heavy Soviet accent that energized America to go down under. Homeowners today continually discover fallouts underneath gardens, behind walls, or in basements when they go to remodel. If you had the money, wouldn't you build a lair to rival Dr. Evil's volcano or Batman's Cave? One <u>guy</u> did to the tune of 15,200 sq feet clocking in at $1.7 million. The cool part, it's in Las Vegas. See some shots from Zillow:

<u>https://www.dailymail.co.uk/news/article-2414497/Most-luxurious-bunker--The-1970s-Cold-War-Era-Home-built-26-feet-underground.html</u>

By the late 70s, Americans started coming around to the belief that a fallout shelter was not going to save them in a nuclear war and came out of hiding. This may explain hippies. Basements remain popular in places with dry weather that aren't near floodplains. In the midwest, basements are considered a standard feature of a home and a necessity for shelter during the wail of a tornado siren.

Basement Doors & Windows Are Pitiful

The first step in basements is finding out if it is practical to have one in your geographical location. The second is to determine its purpose. Once these two questions have been answered, the possibilities of creating an ideal place where you can find sanctuary and usefulness is nearly limitless.

Basements aren't the scary beasts of the past. Basements add significant value to your home, and are excellent sources of income. We are all about diversifying financial portfolios these days. That brings me to the points of entry. We need to discuss basement doors.

One of the fears of basements is feeling entombed, and let's be real, you are enclosed in cement, underground. No matter how ventilated the space is, it's still confining and borderline claustrophobic. Maybe you feel it a little less in the Vegas Bunker of Dreams house above, but I still felt the catacomb breathing at my neck. However a Walkout Basement is a sexy beast.

Walkout basements are the bomb (smirks, see what I did there?). As our journey through basement history has shown us, the purpose of basements have changed through the years. For residential use, the basement has transformed from:

Food storage

↓

Home equipment housing

↓

Storage

↓

Themed rooms

↓

Fallouts

↓

Claustrophobic glorified tombs featuring a variety of rumpus rooms

The next link in this chain should be finished walkout basements. We aren't building bomb shelters anymore and there's nothing that can save us without a government pass. If you don't have a key to the White House, why not enjoy nature from the comfort of your basement.

Creating this kind of dynamic space adds value to the home and shakes off the notion of entombment. There is no way these basements can be considered spooky. Typically, walkout basements are situated on a hill or slope with the main residence above ground level. Walkout basement patios and landscapes provide stunning aesthetics.

Forming your home to the land's topography is an exquisite way to utilize space and pay homage to the nature around you. If your land isn't sloped and you are building from a flat lot, an airy, spacious basement isn't out of the question. For flat lots, a walkup basement may be a solution.

A walkup basement is a basement with an exterior entrance via a stairwell. In older homes, this could be as simple as a bulkhead (cellar) door you pull up to open for stair access. Walkup basements, if done right, add dimension and beauty. Walkup basement renovations involve digging out a bit of space to reveal a wall of the basement. The wall is renovated to include a door, windows, stairs, or sub-terrain patio to open the space up and give the home some personality.

The good news is basement remodels generally pay for themselves. Ask any Realtor, finished is better than unfinished. Your home is the largest investment you will ever make and therefore should yield the largest return. If you have a finished basement, converting it to a walkout or walkup basement will run you less money.

If you are working with an unfinished basement and adding a bathroom and kitchenette, the price will be considerably more. Basement foundation projects alone can cost between $10,000 and $175,000. For the sake of simplicity, we are going to say you have a finished basement and want to convert it to a walkout or walkthrough. There will be excavation involved. This chart from HomeGuide should give you an idea.

BASEMENT EXCAVATION COST

Soil Condition	Cost Per Cubic Yard
Light Soil	$1.65 – $2.18
Moist Soil	$1.96 – $2.64
Wet Soil, Loose Rock	$2.48 – $2.69
Blasted Rock	$3.31

BASEMENT EXCAVATION COSTS BY DIFFICULTY

Depth & Difficulty	Cost Per Square Foot
12' – 18' Depth	$10 – $12
Deeper Footings	$12 – $15
Difficult Soils	$15 – $20

I have looked at several different sites on the costs of a typical walkout basement and the consensus circles the wagons around $47,000 to $100,500 which is about $20,000 more than a regular finished basement due to the extra excavation and grading. The price goes down considerably if the cellar already exists (closer to $12,000). Once the heavy lifting is done and you have a proper dugout, there are some other considerations.

According to <u>HomeAdvisor</u> adding doors and windows for walkout or walkup basements requires a review of the structural integrity, especially if you are cutting through supporting walls. A few Ala Carte Items after excavation are:

- Structural engineers to the tune of about $100-$150 per hour could save you a mint. Usually, structural engineers average out to about $500 per project.

- You can expect framing to cost anywhere from $7-16 per square foot for windows and $350-$800 lump sum for the doorway.

- Waterproofing and sealing is of paramount importance to any exterior project and will be about $80-$200.

- Installation of the exterior door will cost between $2,500-$10,000 depending on more than a few factors.

- If you choose the most popular double patio doors, you are looking at $500-$4500 including labor.

- The patio beyond those beautiful doors will run between $1,750 to $4,750.

The good news, if you aren't using the space, you can always rent it out and pay for the renovation or save up for that cruise to the Bahamas you have been dreaming of with all the VIP bells and whistles. The best side-effect of adding a walkout or walkup basement is the value added to your investment. Finishing a basement gives you a return of 70-75% of your investment. If this remodel isn't in the cards and you are stuck with window wells and an enclosed basement, tricking the mind is the way to go.

Window wells are those U-shaped metal or plastic shoes around a window. They rob the basement of light and a small child can barely squeeze out of them. Cats love them for birthing litters and feline waste. The one use of window wells is draining water away from the foundation.

You can do a few things here to make the basement seem less enclosed. One is to pick a type of window covering, like a heavy drapery, that flows from floor to ceiling to cover the itty bitty window. Or, <u>Biggies Innovations</u> offers window well scenes to trick your mind into believing there is something spectacular outside the window. I was a fan of the Water Wheel.

Either one of these options will make the basement seem a bit brighter and bigger and neither breaks the pocketbook. Paint the walls white and incorporate bright lighting. With more people working from home due to COVID, good lighting is essential or you may have a Joe Versus The Volcano motif going on.

It should not surprise you with the pandemic, the number one home remodel in 2020 and 2021 is the Home-Office. The <u>New York Times</u> ran an article that working and schooling from home were the new normal which led thousands of people to renovate their home to accommodate this new lifestyle.

An overwhelming majority of Americans believe this lifestyle is a permanent change and are calling on a hybrid system of 2 days at an office and 3 days at home if they are unable to work 100% remotely. Some employers will not be filling the commercial office buildings the way they did before COVID. A great many Americans renovated basements into home offices, but a significant number of others repurposed or built office sheds (we take on sheds in another chapter).

Putting The Nail In The Basement Coffin

Basements are the ultimate reflection of a household's purpose. Basements have changed dramatically over the last several decades and capitalizing on space and practicality sits at the heart of architecture and design. It is true that movies, books, and killers may have given basements a bad wrap, but my memories run parallel to the basement from The 70s Show.

COVID hasn't only advanced technology, it has transformed the purpose of a basement for families that have learned to work, school, and play at home. Cabin fever has had the lingering effects of wanting to open up space and bring the outside in to combat the confinement. The best practice is a walkout or walkup basement to capitalize on the space your home affords and increase your sanity by leaps and bounds in the new world.

CHAPTER 9

Just A Little More Wine...Cellar

Good food, great friends, and vintage wine are the essentials for successful social events of the season. The recipe hasn't changed for thousands of years and isn't likely to anytime soon. Wine is a universal delight. How old is wine <u>making</u> (and drinking)? Known and dated artifacts reveal that about 8,000 years ago ancient people were imbibing wine.

The methods of making wine have changed a bit. Those same artifacts also depicted a bunch of men dancing on grapes. About 2,000 years later is when fermentation jars and a wine press blessed the scene, well, cave. Not everyone had grapes year round and had to rely on rice, honey, and other fruits. Wine storage advanced slightly faster, although cave-like conditions are still ideal to keep wine fresh and tasty.

If you look at it, there wasn't much variety in drinks back in the day. You couldn't really walk 5 minutes to the 7-11 or drive down the street to the 2 Starbucks on opposite corners. Wine was made for the moment and consumed on the spot for many years and was traditionally kept in <u>wineskins</u> made of animal skin and clay pots. That is, until a dollar and trade value was placed on wine.

The Greeks called their clay pots Amphorae. Amphorae were transported all over Greece and other regions. The barrels we see in pirate movies didn't start until 100 BC with the Gauls and it wasn't wine; it was fermented beer. This beer storage registered on the disgust meter of the Romans. Romans used glass to drink the wine, but preferred Amphorae to store and pour.

The First Wine Cellars

Incredibly, the first wine cellar was discovered in the city of <u>Tel Kabri</u>. The Canaanite city housed a wine cellar shielding wines from the sun in dark, damp surroundings. The chamber was 40 square meters and filled to the brim with 3-feet tall Amphores. The chamber was adjacent to the dining hall which held lavish parties. Party on Wayne. The chamber was not underground, but was beyond a doubt, a rudimentary wine cellar.

Years later, the Romans *almost* got it right. Romans' wine cellars, called fumantorires, were adjacent to kitchens and on the main floor. These rooms were always billowing smoke on purpose as a preservation method to strangle the oxygen in the room. Smoke also kept the rooms warmer which does not play well with wine properties and accelerated spoilage.

Like some of the best things in life, the first underground Roman wine cellars came by way of a pleasant accident. In need of storage space, some Romans used the family catacombs (underground tombs) to hold their vintage barrels. They inadvertently discovered the secret to wine preservation and it was a game changer.

The massive stone structures of the middle ages required beastly underground support with large arches to distribute the weight of the stone evenly. This architectural design created the perfect environment for wine and the space for storage. The temperature was always cool and there was no light to speak of. The ancient pantry housed grains, vegetables, and wine. It wasn't pretty, but it was practical. If you want pretty, leave it up to the French to fluff it up a bit.

The French were the first to intentionally cultivate wine cellars. Oooo-lala. In the 1600s, they were repurposing Roman mining caves and constructing underground caves to store wine. Word traveled, and shortly after, the caves turned into elaborate showcases of fine wines and a staple for homes across Europe. The French wine cellar was the jumping point for the wine cellars that we have today. The decor has changed, but the requirements of dark and cool have not.

In the finest of restaurants, you can behold the elaborate wine walls and cellars with vintage bottles on display. The prices are not for the faint of heart. Wine cellars are a statement of sophistication, luxury, refinement, culture, and wealth. Not just fast-paced wealth, but the longevity and esteem of generational wealth. In a way, today's wine cellars mimic the hierarchy and stature of parlor rooms explained earlier.

The Wine Cellar Badge of Honor

Wine cellars are considered a luxury room and therefore increase the value of your home and add to the dynamic of prestige and posture. You have arrived. In fact, House Beautiful took a survey of household features that are seen as the largest status symbols of a home and family, top rankings:

1. Wine Cellar
2. Walk-in closet
3. Riding lawn mower
4. Double car garage
5. Wood flooring (Remember, this can be achieved with vinyl)

If you are one of those people that puffs up your chest when someone mentions your beautiful home, a wine cellar is a must-have. Food Network has played a mighty role in the use of wine and wine cellars with cooking shows infusing alcohol with cooking and creative drinks. Wine use went from 449 million gallons a year to 913 gallons shortly after the network's release. The use of wine is a cultural and cooking staple and leads to impressive, fancy wine rooms inching ever closer to a desired amenity, like the TV room. Ironically, wine rooms with stone walls (sound familiar) are the most popular.

Since wine cellars add value and status to homes, even non-wine drinkers are opting to have them as a feature in their homes. Throwing wine tasting parties are an excellent way to socialize and impress the boss and coworkers. Or, fool them into believing you are sophisticated and worldly while really you are hiding the box wine in the garage refrigerator. Appearances matter in time and place.

Why Have A Wine Cellar

If you truly enjoy wine and it isn't just for show (you drink alone), having a <u>wine cellar</u> in the home has plenty of bonus benefits. One being that wines are perishable and need a controlled temperature. The refrigerator is not controlled and they vibrate. Vibration is not good for wine. Don't play with your wine until you are ready to drink it. Wine cellars control both temperature and humidity giving wine the ideal climate to grow in taste and value.

Another benefit of having a cellar is you can purchase high quality wine when it is being offered at a lower price because you have the means to store it. Also, if you have surprise guests pop in, or you run out of wine, there is no 'beer run' necessary. You have ample supply without losing quality or theme; party like a boss.

There is the matter of collecting and organizing if you have OCD like me. I'm not a wine collector, I am a baseball card collector. If you think about it, baseball card collecting and wine have several of the same challenges and joys in storage, organization, socialization, showcasing, collection preferences, investment, pride, and stature. Both types of collecting have long and short-game goals.

If I collected wine, it would undoubtedly be listed in Excel and color-coded in inventory like my cards. There is a love of collecting and organizing that is shown through the care that a display (wine cellar) is created. Dare I say, it's fun? Yup.

Having a wine cellar educates you about the wine you drink and the wine you collect. You will gain a wealth of knowledge and expertise on the old and current events in the industry. Wine will tell you it's secrets and that makes for great stories at parties if you usually don't know how to break the ice or know what to say.

You will also find yourself in a new circle of friends doing interesting things. Make room for the members only jacket in the closet. Wine is an investment and a lifestyle. Having a wine cellar is cost-effective and practical.

Not every wine cellar is created equal. Some are large rooms and others are small and cozy. The key thing here is that the wine is protected and the cellar functions as intended. There are a number of different ways to add a wine cellar or cabinet to your home depending on your budget. If you Google wine cellars, there will be cabinets, walls, coolers, etc. Here, we are talking about an actual ROOM.

So, How Much Are We Talking?

Several sites on the internet will quote you anywhere from $5,000 to $150,000 to add a wine cellar to your home. <u>Home Advisor</u> says the average is about $40,000 for a walk-in wine cave. The price ranges dramatically from low to high due to the location that is chosen. If you already have subterranean space, then you need not start from scratch; and that matters. Big time.

Custom cabinetry can be another huge cost; however some cabinets are as low as $500 and if you are handy, you can do alot yourself. Creating a wine cellar on a budget is entirely possible and highly encouraged. A room can hold about 3,000 bottles of wine. Maybe that is overzealous for your lifestyle, so space can be easily adjusted to fit your needs. You can even utilize space that we have previously cleared out in this book; say like, under the stairs.

As with any build, the cost is going to fluctuate on space and materials. Remember, the primary goal is functionality. Cute won't cut it. Cellars range between 25 and 150 square feet. It is important to consider your needs, practicality, functionality, materials and how this relates to your budget. Some things to think about:

- Size & Location
- Design & Layout
- Storage capacity & Rack material
- Refrigeration & Humidity
- Lighting

When considering these features and what works for you, the optimum solution will start to present itself. Some options are:

Underfloor: This is a pull up or automatic system built directly under the floor or underground. Think of it similar to a pool with a retractable cover of cement. Basketball course by day, pool by night. In this case, the living room floor by day, wine cave by night. Personally, I have never seen one of these and I would consider this a half-ass kind of a thing, but that's just me. It doesn't really scream WINE LOVER.

Basement: Now we are talking. If you already have a basement, the best solution in my mind is to convert a small section into a wine cellar. I love basements, they are so versatile. In this case, you can commit to a stellar cellar between $10 to $25,000.

Under the Stairs: This is really a great way to use space beneath the stairs. Wine is better than old musty boxes any day of the week. The challenge here would be vibrations and fluctuating temperatures. Plus, under the stairs is not like four square corners, custom racks will be needed to complete the layout.

Walk-in Closet: As a woman, this is a hard NO. I need my shoe space. But, if you are a single dude who doesn't need 2 walk-ins; this may work. Remember, not every room needs a closet; but a home needs a wine cellar. Kill 2 birds with one stone here. It is not likely your closet has sunlight invading the space.

These are just a few locations. If you prefer wine to food, you could always look at the pantry. It is also important to remember that the increased value a wine cellar adds is because it is pleasing to the eye. Design is of paramount importance and right up there with functionality. Things to consider in design:

Spiral: Small spiral cabinets that pull up and are best for underfloor and small spaces.

Tasting Room: If you have a small wine cellar, having a tasting room will make it seem bigger and plush because tasting rooms need not be insulated but are part of a wine cellar feature. A decorative tasting room can add massive street credit to your cellar.

Storage capacity should be decided well before the build. Not every wine requires refrigeration so understanding that is key as well. Non-refrigerated wines are usually kept in a storage cabinet nearby or in the tasting room. Knowing this fact may change your space and insulation cost requirements completely.

Once you have your plan sketched out with your specific needs, cost is easy to figure out. Remember to leave a little room in the budget for a humidor. They go hand in hand with black tie parties and add style as a lavish, old-money feel, piece of furniture. Wine cellar additions are within reach, it is the dusting that keeps me from doing it. When I can afford to pay someone to clean, that is the day I will have a wine cellar.

CHAPTER 10

Forget Front Yards

Front yards are private strips of publicly experienced property and vary depending on where you live. Vermont enjoys the largest lots in America, while California and Nevada enjoy the smallest. Enjoy may be an overstatement. Front yards are a point of contention among neighbors and have been for years. Here are some facts:

- 91% of <u>Americans</u> want to live in a community where they see nice landscaping
- 71% of your neighbors care about how *your* front yard looks
- 85% of Americans say that landscape is a deciding factor in purchasing a home
- 44% want to **customize** their front yard space

In that 44% is our point of contention in defining what a front yard should be. Opinions are like assholes, everybody has one. The truth of the matter is, in some areas, city ordinances govern most of that 44% and kick their individuality and creative land usage to the curb, literally.

Homeowners have little say in the planning and development of their front yard thanks to Euclidean Zoning. In 1926, there was a landmark Supreme Court case that, in a nutshell, allowed township municipalities to divide a town into zones based on their permitted uses. Permitted uses are things like:

- Commercial
- Residential
- Industrial

And within these zones, further restrictions and guidelines are issued in the form of ordinances, including setbacks. Setbacks dictate how far your structure must be from the curb, or property line, or your neighbor, among other things, and are the guidelines home developers must follow while creating planned communities, including your front yard.

Now that we have provided the origin story for the basics of urban planning and development that came into play when your house was designed, let's find out who is to blame for the front yard and why this archaic waste of space is still here.

Who Started Front Yards Anyway?

Originally, front yards started in European and French castles. The aristocrats would keep the yard mowed down, using free-range cattle, so they could see enemy troops coming and avoid ambush. Lawn is an English word 'launde,' meaning an opening in the woods, which is where castles were built. But how did this travel to America? I mean, we aren't exactly known for our historic castles along the countryside.

In 17th century France, the Versailles gardens was famous with its green carpet inspiring the elite across several regions to design well-manicured gardens and grass in their front lawns. Mind you, these front lawns were actually acreages taking immense human and animal resources to maintain, the cost of which made a well-groomed lawn a status symbol.

Enter the Industrial Revolution, again. With the Industrial Revolution, the world saw its first lawn mower in 1830, this was a game changer. By the 19th century, manpower for front yards was yesterday's news because lawn mowers were accessible to everyone. But that wasn't the only thing extending the green carpet across America. There was a perfect <u>storm</u> brewing:

- Public park movement
- Using automobiles for commuting and distance travel vs. trains
- The federal government financed6 low-cost mortgages after WWII, encouraging tract homes with front lawns to mimic middle-class suburbia

The guy that designed Central Park in New York, Frederick Law Olmstead, became the father of American landscape design. He also was responsible for designing the suburbs. Olmstead's vision was for each house to have a front lawn; the dude really liked parks. At the same time that he was developing these personal Edens in suburbia, people were being overrun by the industrial revolution and fled to the suburbs for sanctuary. The supply and demand module was thriving.

Families wanted to move from the cities and its noise riddled concrete to a sanctuary of velvety green, chirping birds, and peaceful living to raise children. Families thanked the Industrial Revolution for the lawn mowers and frolicked off into wild suburbia. Suburbia made front yards famous across the nation, but it did not give front yards the stigma that a later community did.

The evil of front lawns was handed down by Abraham Levitt (the first Karen) in the late 1940s. He founded Levittown (and an apparent narcissist), which was declared the ideal American suburbia. You can think of this as the very first Homeowners Association. The diabolical genius of Levittown community was:

- The lawns were already in place when the new owner moved in
- The homeowner was given a pamphlet about the importance of maintaining the perfect lawn
- Tips about how to keep the lawn lush, green, and weed-free were explained, sternly

There you have it, folks, yard regulations with your entire community acting as judge, jury, and executioner. Why? There was written documentation in the form of a pamphlet, and if you didn't follow it, you were the community asshole. Peer pressure is the weapon of a finely manicured suburb. The philosophy from a page in his <u>book</u>:

"...is to attain a patch of green grass of a singular type with no weeds that is attached to your home. It should be no more than an inch and a half tall, and neatly edged. This means you must be willing to care for it. It must be watered, mowed, repaired, and cultivated."

That's more than a bit intimidating, like spoken straight from the Principal's mouth. Levittown had 30,000 people tour its model homes in the opening weekend. They became so popular across the country that as a side-effect of this celebration of uniformity, grass lawns became the standard and were cookie-cut into every perfect grid of every suburb. Thanks to Levittown:

- Nearly 80% of all homes in the US have grass lawns taking more water than wheat and corn do every year (that's food)
- Each year, 3 billion hours are spent on mowing lawns

Thus began the struggle of the urban front yard flex keeping neighbors pitted in friendly competition against neighbors for hundreds of years.

The Psychology Of The Front Yard

From 1957 to 1963, there was a sitcom about a naive, somewhat curious child and his wholesome adventures through suburbia. Mom handled the household chores in heels and pearls, and dad walked through the door just in time for a martini and dinner. The name of the show was Leave It To Beaver (the child being 'the Beaver'). Yeah, I laughed too.

This show was the epitome of the good fun, 'golly-gee' life where everyone knew their place, and everything was in its place. This is what the American family in suburbia was supposed to be, what they wanted to be. The perceived life of families in the suburbs had a profound effect across America of being the perfect life, and it embedded itself deeply in our psyche.

In 1998, Jim Carrey starred in a movie called The Truman Show, where a corporation purchased a baby (Carrey) and, as an experiment and expression of love, created a Levittown-mirrored suburban paradise where the baby was raised by actors and actresses playing the part of friends and family. The caveat, cameras were on him 24/7, so the viewers could watch him grow up, and he didn't know any of it. He was trapped in the American dream.

If you want to be really disturbed, watch Stepford Wives. Suburban life is a mindset that has stood the test of time and instilled itself in our minds and hearts as the perfect life, a legacy. Believe it or not, there are <u>museums</u> dedicated to the well-preserved artifacts of 'the burbs.' So, even in Truman's 1998 fantasy, which was well over 30 years later, when you say perfect neighborhood, it is the 1950s suburbs that come to mind. That trend carries on 70 years later. Why?

<u>Suburbs</u> provide a false sense of security because you are surrounded by like-minded individuals bonded in community. You know each other. The familiarity bonds into a feeling of protection and safety. You feel like you belong.

Gated communities intensify false senses of security in keeping the 'undesirables' out. By undesirables, I mean renters. Homeownership brings a sense of pride in what you have accomplished, and suburbia fears the renter culture because it is not known for a permanently vested interest in community.

Suburbs aren't about religion, sex, or race. Suburbs are a diverse culture caring for what they own, investing in it; and that cultivates respect for other people's things. People in suburbia feel that care in and for the community is a safety net from vandalism and crime. This is why if your neighbors front yard is a chaotic mess, it reflects poorly on the entire neighborhood because uniformity demonstrates similar interest, and conformity is its mechanism.

Neighborhood Watch gives absolute authority (ask anyone on the team) to maddog your kids' friends when they enter the community because they are 'unknowns.' Why? Because kids aren't equipped with the life lessons to know how hard you worked to have that front yard and are therefore a threat with $200 sneakers that could damage a blade of grass at any moment.

Unless you have lived in a suburban neighborhood and experienced it firsthand, you will never understand the safety in numbers, cohesion, and conformity. Homeowners Associations have upheld their end of the bargain and graduated from a pamphlet to an enormous 3-ring binder of governing documents called Codes, Covenants, and Restrictions (CCRs). Sounds authoritative and severe right? It sometimes is. They can foreclose on your home (more on that later).

Governing documents are lists of the do and do-nots of your home and the neighborhood. Some of these are codified into law and city ordinances, others are nuisance rules of the HOA to preserve the integrity and the aesthetic value (conformity), and you can be heavily fined if you are not in compliance.

The interesting thing is you don't need to sign anything. You are automatically enrolled as a member of the association and subject to the CCRs the day you purchase your home. You passively agree to all of the subsequent rules and regulations. One of them is caring for your front yard, which your home undoubtedly came equipped with to perpetuate the lifestyle of the suburbs. Consequently, your backyard is in there too.

The Green People

Some people have been attempting to get creative with their front yards rather than just have grass or rock run across them. Bathrooms and front lawns may not have changed since the 1950s, but the world around it certainly has.

Being energy-efficient and 'green' (sustainability) has been taken to a new level, and attention has recently been turned to the front yard. Damn those pesky ordinances and governing documents. A <u>couple</u> in Florida won their 6-year battle to plant some vegetables in their front yard. In Michigan, criminal charges were filed where a woman faced 93 <u>days</u> in jail for a vegetable garden in the front lawn; when you say that out loud, it's even more ridiculous.

Not that I agree with people growing things in their front lawns, I think it's tacky, and that's what backyards are for. But jail time? Or the time, energy, and money that went into a 6-year court battle over vegetables. It's asinine. We are spending more money on the problem than the solution.

The Smart Growth Development Principle

Massachusetts legislation recently passed a <u>law</u> focusing on implementing mixed land use. The law promotes affordable housing initiatives and invites collaboration from homebuilders and developers. The law is known as the smart growth development principle.

Massachusetts realized that changing from a Euclidean zoning platform will not be immediate and instead proposed to integrate small changes with new development focus by introducing elements to existing developments. Simply put - baby-steps.

The state is looking to have communities revise and amend zoning laws to more easily incorporate smart growth practices. One of these objectives is to regulate land use but not prohibit land use. For example, if you want a wrap-around front porch and not a front yard, the planning office would provide the guidelines on how to build the wrap-around porch rather than prohibit the act altogether.

Special use permits allow for flexibility and provide incentives to break preexisting conformity and promote a partnership between developers and community. This is a radical change compared to the Euclidean zoning platform that has run unchecked for years.

The Art Of Forgetting About It

What if we could remove the deeply-embedded need for the white-picket-fence that has been forced into the American psyche? In truth, a majority may suffer withdrawal from the abrupt culture shock, but with change comes growth. There is a passage from the <u>Chicago</u> Tribune that sticks in my mind:

The American front lawn, the postage stamp of grass spread before a set-back house, the stage upon which you display status, the frame inside which you project taste, that one-time signifier of leisure that came to suck up leisure time, is increasingly seen as a waste.

Boom. They summed up in one sentence the entire topic of this Chapter. Millennials are moving into suburbs in droves to escape cities and sequester inside their homes to worship technical devices, or whatever it is that Millennials do. The main difference with Millennials from prior generations is: they don't see front lawns as a sign of status.

We, as a nation, have started questioning our historical beliefs in their entirety to the point of gross extremes from historical monuments to identifying as a unicorn. Society is in the midst of waves of change in fitting form to function. Why not include front yards in this revolution?

The stigma of a content life that once gripped the philosophy of a front yard is vanishing. Front yards simply don't mean what they used to and have lost their value. The extension of front yards as a social contract to your community is over. Just as monuments are seen as a sign of repression by some, so is the destiny of the manicured front yard.

American culture is changing from the sunny outdoors to retreating in the warm glow of laptops, Sony PlayStations, smartphones, and other devices. In the 1950s, your neighborhood was your world. Now the world has expanded exponentially at your fingertips.

How The Rest Of The World Does It

In our exposure to other cultures and places in the world with all of this technology, it should not surprise you that most other countries have <u>extinguished</u> the use of a front yard. They have suburbs with large, luscious, private backyards but NO front yard.

Front yard inspirations traveled here on French wings, so it is utterly ironic that they were one of the first countries to see how redonkulous and tedious front yards were. It was explained in Paris at: <u>https://www.gardenrant.com/2013/01/no-front-yard.html</u>

Setback areas have been enclosed by walls, fences or hedges, and made into functional patios ornamented by planter boxes. A spacious and private yard lies behind the home. There are no rear alleys. This simple design, of which there must be hundreds of thousands of examples in Paris alone, would be illegal under every American zoning code.

France isn't the only front yard revolutionary; many other countries don't have them anymore. Remember the bloody Romans? Here's a dose of their front yard philosophy:

https://www.gardenrant.com/2013/01/no-front-yard.html

Setbacks are entirely occupied by patios. Backyards are put to productive use as personal vegetable gardens with large balconies above. There is zero turf lawn to be found.

America is the infant in the history of how long a civilization has been around, but trends often do roll our way when we aren't the ones trending them. The problem with America embracing a no front yard trend is that city codes in the US require setbacks; we have no choice until the regulations are forced to change.

Funny, isn't it? The history of populations fleeing to America for freedom from religious persecution and to exercise the enjoyment of their land, yet we continually create codes and governing documents restricting those same enjoyments. America constantly seeks sustainability and efficiency but doesn't create the breathing room necessary to accomplish the goal.

How A City Ordinance Works

Since ordinances are created in individual cities and townships to cater to specific population areas, it can be said no two cities are alike. Meaning, if you don't like the restrictions on your house, move outside of those restrictions into a more accommodating area, or there is the other option.

The Supreme Court saw that any zoning ordinances made by the local legislature can be appealed and simultaneously can attempt to be changed. They handed down reasons as to why some ordinances should be changed:

"Common validity challenges, which are described further in this report, include spot zoning, fair share, exclusionary, substantive due process, irrationality, and equal protection."

If you are a homeowner affected by a city ordinance, you can appeal. Changing a local ordinance requires:

- The governing body (Board of appeals, different names per city)
- Planning agency
- Petition by affected property owners

A public hearing regarding the proposed change must take place by the planning agency/governing body with proper notice posted and published. Riveting discussions will take place between the board and the population that attends this meeting.

Then, the Amendment must get a majority vote of the governing body. If successful, an Amendment to the Ordinance will be written to cite the specific changes. As a homeowner, you can ask for a variance, which is close to the same process.

Introducing the APA: American Planning Association

The American Planning Association (APA) is an organization that not only guides and educates on urban planning but empowers homeowners to have a voice and participate in the process.

The APA is aware that changing city ordinances to reflect the times is necessary. Ordinances should be developed as living laws fluctuating with the demand and need of the social climate while maintaining basic provisions and guidelines to prevent chaos. The APA states:

"It is obvious that provisions must be made for changing the regulations as conditions change or new conditions arise. Otherwise zoning would be a "strait-jacket" and a detriment to a community instead of an asset."

<u>Membership</u> is open to anyone. You will be provided with their Planning magazine keeping you in the know with how communities are being planned and the issues developing within your local communities. The membership dues are about $80 per year and worth the voice and information you receive in being a member. If you are concerned about how irresponsible and out of control urban planning has become, this is the place to start.

The APA is an authoritative agency that:

- Municipalities look to for guidance and procedure
- Courts look to for Amicus Briefs (opinions on how to handle a dispute)
- Professionals get their education from
- Residents can participate in the molding of current and inspiration of future neighborhoods and home development

Their advocacy group believes in being proactive rather than reactive to improve communities and practices. Understanding and participating in the planning process is the momentum influencing change and inspires progress, including your front yard.

CHAPTER 11

Baby's Got A Big Backyard

Much like the kitchen is the heart of a home, the backyard is the vital organ of outdoor living. Backyards across the nation feature patios, decks, sprawled lawn furniture in organized chaos, outdoor kitchens, swimming pools, and playgrounds. Backyards are where we relax, work, celebrate, and play. We enjoy the fruits of our labor in private edens or open them up for exclusive social gatherings and barbecue parties.

Homes with pristine, finished landscaping enjoy a significant price point value compared to those with unfinished yards. Large lots are sought after by home buyers because they promise a stunning sanctuary and individuality within a residential district of close proximity. Fire up any google search of 'what should a backyard have' and you will be bombarded with endless lists featuring entertainment and items for fantastical backyard soirees.

So why, in the name of all that is holy, do builders not equip homes with adequate electrical and plumbing fixtures to enjoy the outdoors? Are we savages? It seems every remodel requires significant reach around to pull the veins from inside the home to the outdoors. Careful though, some HOAs whisper heated threats into your ear about deadlines. The foreplay sucks and it costs too much.

In a day and age where technology is fused inside every smart home, why not give homeowners the tools to shape leisure areas how they like? A home is our castle! At a minimum, homes should come standard with:

- A fence
- A patio
- An outdoor kitchen (or at a minimum, the hookups)
- A grassy area
- Ample electrical & plumbing connects

This is mandatory backyard bone structure. The homeowner can beef it up affordably from there. These staples for backyards reflect the era and lifestyle we have propagated for decades. Backyards have changed with the flow of society throughout history. Sustainability plays a large part (hence the grassy area for you gardners out there) but enjoyment and quality time are prominent as well. This wasn't always so.

The Business End of a Backyard

American backyards in the pre-World War II <u>era</u> were reserved to supply the household economy with sustenance. Food was the name of the game, including livestock and its bounty. Often the backyard was split between gardens and equipment storage for a host of specialty craft trades. It was the ideal place of the king of thrones--the outhouse (we get into this later). The backyard delight was frosted in practicality and commerce, not enjoyment and leisure, but still a vital part of home real estate.

Americans were devoted to self-sufficiency and sustainability. Remember root cellars? This is when food storage peaked. The birthplace of hoarding. After the war, a swarm of activity with the industrial revolution came into play. America invested in infrastructures, highways, and suburbs. The GI Bill was a monumental buffer to get an education, start a business, and buy a home. The message transformed from FRUGAL to SPEND, SPEND, SPEND--and the economy rebounded with the quickness.

Supermarkets peppered the landscape in the 1950s and 60s. As a result, food storage shifted indoors and people were introduced to technology making life easier and diminished time-consuming chores out of many areas of our lives. The result? America had quality leisure time, more backyard space, and money to spend. Life was good. Consumer culture was hopping to the tune of relaxation. Backyards nestled into the high-achiever, accomplished status of the American Dream.

Americans carved out staging areas for backyard leisure palaces in the form of decks and patios. Since supermarkets were readily available, dirt gardens were replaced with grassy knolls in the center of lush landscape for badminton and croquet. Homeowners customized their backyards in personality, showing off their playful hobbies, styles, and interests - seducing social interactions far and wide.

In ancient times, there were public baths. America scooped up this ideology and planted pools in the backyard. You had arrived when your backyard encompassed a classic kidney-shaped suburban swimming hole. Social opportunities are the business end of a backyard now. Backyards were for play. Where there is play, there are nosy neighbors.

Fences Make Good Neighbors

If you watched TV in the 90s, you stumbled across Wilson. Dr. Wilson was Tim 'The Toolman' Taylor's fence lurking neighbor on the series Home Improvement. Wilson was a source of wisdom, advice, and meaningful quotes throughout the show. He was Tim Taylor's Yoda figure, the perfect neighbor--and stayed behind the fence.

Unlike front yards, which should not have a fence, backyards should because they are a private sanctum, not the public introduction to your home. Fences serve several purposes and should be standard for homebuilding. Let's clarify that, quality fences, not the posts of stray driftwood with duct tape around the perimeter. Fences should match the aesthetic of your home and add value. Some of the perks are:

<u>Security & Safety</u> - Fences are a deterrent. If you drop a $100 bill in public and walk away vs. dropping $100 bill in your backyard, the odds of you finding the $100 you lost increase dramatically in a private setting. The same goes for your stuff.

The one who dies with the most toys wins is the mantra of American culture. Sad, but true. We are compulsive overconsumers. If you see your neighbor's kids having fun on a trampoline, your children will bully you into getting a trampoline--that's life. Fences provide a layer of protection and privacy. Crime is everywhere and fences serve as a precautionary measure.

Fences are ideal in keeping things in and out. Dogs, pets, and children 'in'; wild suburban predators, like trespassers and solicitors 'out'. I feel safer letting my kids out to play knowing they are contained and not able to wander out into the street or walk away with a passerby.

Prancing Nekkid - Privacy is the number one reason people install fences. If you like prancing around naked in the backyard collecting butterflies, I don't judge, but I don't want my kids to see it either, so, I thank you. Tall bushes and trees serve as excellent privacy buffers and compliment your fence.

Aesthetics - Curb appeal is critical when selling your home. Fences elevate curb appeal and raise value simultaneously. The important thing is choosing the right fence that echoes the look of your home. Something that clashes will obviously have the opposite effect. Homebuyers look for security, privacy, and curb appeal.

Boundaries - Knowing what you own is important in keeping polite banter up with the neighbors. There has been more than one horror story written about stray branches of a tree spewing leaves across lot lines. Installing a fence along the boundary ensures there are no disputes of who owns what and keeps things friendly.

Finding the right kind of fencing for your home's personality can be a challenge. Most people select what they see around the community. Fences can be way more exciting than that. One of my favorites - shutter fencing.

This is probably one of the coolest DIY projects I have ever seen; however, people can manipulate the shutters to see in. If you want to completely eliminate peepability, I suggest a full wall fence with added shelving to add a little flavor.

This type of fence adds stature and luxury to any backyard, not to mention complete privacy. Or, maybe you want your backyard to emanate that your home is your castle. In that case, a sound wall would be ideal.

Sound walls provide a sense of nature with privacy and security. Many people incorporate waterfalls and ponds into their wall for a sanctuary that rivals monk gardens in Tibet.

These are just a few examples that show fence-shopping can be incredibly fun and enlightening. Backyards are a showcase for your personality and interests. Fences are a huge part of that. Depending on the fence you choose, prices to install the fence will vary. According to <u>HomeGuide</u>, 2021 fence pricing looks something like this:

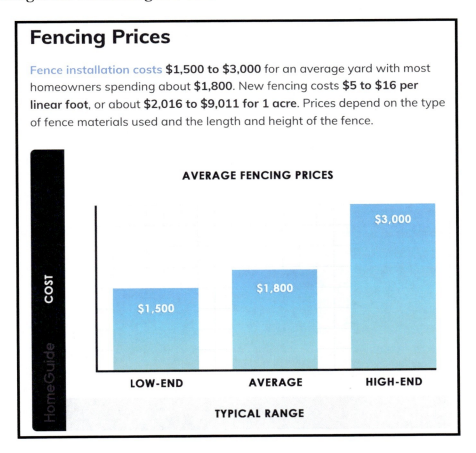

You can purchase the fencing and install it yourself to save costs. There is always an option of repurposing material you have to create a unique privacy fence. Unfortunately, restrictions on fencing are regulated by HOAS (Homeowner Associations) if you live in one, which we get into later. Now that the fence is up, let's talk about decks and patios.

Patios-The Backyard Hangout

The backyard is a place of leisure, so having some type of seating is crucial. The seating area doesn't have to be on the ridiculously expensive side. Seating should convey a message when people enter the space, something like:

I'm about to relax in the outdoorsy coziness and enjoy a drink with good company.

Even though you are in the backyard, the continuity should flow from indoor to outdoor and appear less of a division and more of an extension. Think of it like an outdoor room. This is why builders need to stop with the dirt lot and give homebuyers some standard options, including a patio or deck.

Continuity blends the scene and provides consistency while capitalizing on the space available. Why is it important to start putting a real investment into our outdoor habitats? Because the <u>majority</u> of Americans have become cave dwellers and it isn't good. It seems we have de-evolutionized in a way.

The Environmental Protection Agency (EPA), completed a study finding the average American spends 93% of life indoors. In case you missed it, that's the equivalent of half a day per week outside. People are becoming unhealthy and brittle because of it. Here's a few more facts:

- Concentrations of pollutants are 2-5X higher indoors
- Staying inside increases your likelihood of cold & flu due to the higher concentrations of pollutants
- Spending more time outdoors is linked to better moods and a better outlook on life, including increased self-esteem

These findings correlate with generational depression stats being on the rise since the mid-90s and piggybacks on the new COVID lifestyle. How we equip our homes not only benefits our investment, it benefits our quality of life and health. Architecture is often a reflection of the times. Today's time calls for increased outdoor living and the easiest way to accommodate the need is a robust backyard plan with a few standard amenities.

Backyard space is being reimagined to align with sustainability and maximize use of space while receiving a return of value and enjoyment. According to <u>HomeAdvisor</u>, the cost for a new patio will look something like this:

Cost to Put in a New Patio by Size

7 X 7	$250-$2,500
10 X 10	$500-$5,000
12 X 12	$750-$7,200
16 X 18	$1,450-$14,500
20 X 20	$2,000-$20,000

This cost varies depending on what material you use, if you need a walkway, or if you add a firepit, etc. This depicts the national average cost. If you have a smaller size budget, simple can be extremely elegant. Overhead shelter along with heating and cooling functions in the outdoors should be a consideration. Depending where you live, there are several feasible outdoor solutions from misters to standalone propane heaters.

Practicality and purpose can easily be accomplished to suit your personality and lifestyle. The goal is to get outside and be healthy and happy in your leisure time. This is why outdoor kitchens are a staple in today's homes.

Outdoor Kitchens-What's Cooking?

Back when I was kicking around the same 9 blocks in the neighborhood, there was nothing like the smell of grilling meat. Once one person started, it was a chain reaction for the rest of the neighborhood to dorn their 'Kiss The Chef' aprons and head to the backyard. The firing up of backyard grills could be compared to 'the wave' at football games--with more enthusiasm.

Outdoor kitchens should be a staple in every backyard to accompany the fence and patio--the trifecta of a good time. Although outdoor kitchens sound a bit extravagant, they don't need to be. Outdoor kitchens that offer practicality and increase your time outdoors have many benefits and are a fun, affordable DIY project.

According to the <u>BBQ Guys</u>, there are 5 minimum essential elements an outdoor kitchen should have:

1. Built-in gas grill
2. Access doors
3. Side burner
4. Compact refrigerator
5. Trash bin

This simple recipe of accessories will have you cooking in no time and there are plenty of ways to personalize the space. The best part, a big area isn't necessary. Now, of course if you have the room and want to go big or go home, something like this is ideal:

<u>https://williamsonsource.com/the-ultimate-pool-luxury-outdoor-kitchen-and-living-space/</u>

A robust outdoor kitchen ensemble often includes:

- Pizza ovens
- Wine fridge
- Running water
- Smoker
- Fire pit
- Flat grill; and
- Counterspace

Generally, you do not need a building permit for an outdoor kitchen's construction. However, you will most likely need one for the electrical and plumbing work. Outdoor kitchens can range anywhere from $2,200 to $15,000 depending on the appliances you select and whether you choose to hire specialists or are handy and can do it yourself.

There are plenty of <u>reasons</u> to turn your backyard into a day/night out for family and friends by adding a mandatory outdoor kitchen to home design. We already pointed out cave dweller symptoms, but here are a few others.

Increases Home Value - Installing an outdoor kitchen helps your home sell for 30% more than listing price. Home amenities and the style of your design profoundly impact the sales price of your home and attract eager buyers. CNN Money, About.com, and Remodeling Magazine are advocates for outdoor kitchens and indicate the average return on investment is 100-200%.

Creates a Social Paradise - COVID has made major strides in making us seek out our own entertainment and starved us for interaction. This may be the one thing that boomers and millennials have in common. BOTH are willing to pay more than $5,000 for an attractive outdoor living space. The boomer appeal is in grilling and the millennial appeal is in outdoor games. For once, it is a perfect marriage.

Increases the Amount of Living Space - The transition from indoor to outdoor flows smoothly and allows for repurposed space to be used to its full potential for our enjoyment. Function and form can make outdoor spaces uber-efficient. An outdoor set of kitchenware and a dishwasher makes cleaning up a breeze. Living outdoors offers more entertainment and living space to prevent overcrowding.

Gracious Cooking Room - If you have experienced tight quarters in a kitchen during Thanksgiving where everyone is playing chef to their main dish--I feel your pain. Outdoor kitchens provide elbow room for family and social gatherings. Especially with a kitchen island. There is enough room to deep fry a turkey and participate in day drinking with a spacious counter bar. A refrigerator outdoors means everyone can store their goodies. If there are spills, hose it down. Perfecto!

Money Saving - Outdoor kitchens save money in a few ways: Utilities and Eating Out. When the kitchen gets cooking, the air conditioner is forced to accommodate for the sizzling heat. Having the kitchen outdoors saves the utility boost. Taking the extended family out for dinner can be expensive. Outdoor kitchens bring the entertainment of eating out to you in a relaxed atmosphere. Pop up a screen and watch movies in the backyard. Many expensive night-out activities can be replicated and improved upon in your backyard.

A Patch of Grass and Gardens Are Banging

The sustainability of home economy and conservation gardening has become of paramount importance when faced with the lack of toilet paper and food industry items in recent years. Crowdfunded community <u>gardens</u> and Victory Gardens are being revitalized throughout the United States. Leah Penniman, a co-director and farming manager at Soul Fire Farm indicated:

"We can't fundamentally have freedom and autonomy and dignity and community power without some measure of control of our food systems," Penniman said. "I think this gardening interest arises from a visceral understanding of that truth."

The truth is, even <u>before</u> the pandemic, numbers of gardeners were climbing in 2015; spending nearly $6 billion in the gardening space. The interesting thing, yes, there were boomers, but 18-34 year olds participated in gardening expenditures and enjoyment. Millenials are committed to sustainability for the long-haul. <u>Squarefootgardening.org</u> has been helping thousands of people garden while using very little space.

The 2020 recession and COVID were the perfect storm for new gardening hobbyists to enter the arena fulfilling a need for food security. The last comparable surge took place during World War II as you remember from our prepper chapter. What wasn't highlighted in that chapter are the many <u>benefits</u> of gardening:

- Gardening is therapeutic and has a positive impact on health and wellness
- Gardening at home or in a community garden serves as an antidepressant
- People are less depressed outdoors and gardening promotes talk-therapy
- Outdoor time increases vibes in good mood, sociability, and energy
- Gardening improves attention and cognition skills
- Gardening feeds our 'nature/nurture' soul leading to increased self-worth and societal contributions
- Their is proof letting physical wounds 'air out' speeds the healing process

- Saves money on consumer foods and is better for you
- Cures boredom and provides physical fitness

A survey by <u>Miracle-Gro</u> showed 55% of Americans are gardening or caring for their lawn during the pandemic. The reasons for doing so align with the benefits for GenZ, GenX, and Millenials:

- 54% Do it to stay busy
- 48% Feel a sense of accomplishment
- 48% To reduce stress
- 33% Access to fresh food; and
- 49% Say they are spending more time outdoors than before the outbreak

Experts believe gardening is not only here to stay, but will continue to grow. Younger generations have picked up the hobby. What does that tell us? That a patch of grass should be mandatory in the backyard from home developers. Homebuyers can opt to install a play area, start a food garden, or advocate for conservation.

There is a wildlife gardening movement flowing across the country. Millions are creating <u>eco-friendly</u> spaces to relax, rejuvenate, and invite the birds and the bees--literal birds and bees. Some people are creating habitats on patios, porches, or window sills. According to the National Gardening Survey & University of New Hampshire for the National Wildlife Federation:

- Over the last 3 years, 64.1 million Americans (1 in 4) purchased a plant that benefits birds, bees, or butterflies
- 23.1 million Americans converted part of their lawn to natural/wildflower landscape in 2019
- A majority of Americans are spending more on organic lawn and gardening products

Interestingly, the National Wildlife Federation partnered with Taylor Morrison (the 5th largest homebuilder in the country) to certify 8,000+ acres of open space as wildlife habitat within its developments. An overwhelming majority of this nation wants a mandatory grass patch and the hookups to care for it.

This Century Requires Outdoor Utility Access

We have discussed the basic backyard arsenal that should come standard in home building:

- Fence
- Patio
- Outdoor Kitchen
- Grassy Area

The remaining standard pieces are the veins that keep the heart of the backyard pumping. It is impossible to efficiently run a backyard economy without adequate electricity and plumbing. Granted, an outdoor kitchen should come with the necessary gas lines and ample electrical outlets, but that is not the end all be all.

The backyard should not look like a parking lot theme park with cables and wires forming an electrified web on the ground. Attempting to enjoy yourself while tripping over the backyard network isn't feasible, safe, or childproof.

To enjoy the outdoors, there is lighting, speakers, TVs, and any number of entertainment options and accessories available. Homeowners are hosting birthday parties, weddings, and other events in their backyard more and more. It is easier to equip the backyard while the home is being built vs. attempting to pull out the necessary utilities during a home renovation. It's shenanigans!

Most homeowners have utilities running underground they don't know about and 50% of homeowners don't call the utility companies (call 811) to check before digging. This can be hazardous and more than a pain in the ass. Marking utilities can be as easy as creating gnome outlets or using other yard creatures and critters so homeowners know where the lines are and can use them. Not knowing where they are can, and does, result in death.

Sewer line marker

Zombie (named Herb) marks my sewer line; why can't we use critters like this for electricity, etc?

For example, this is a picture of my backyard. Herb, our zombie, marks the sewer line. We marked it because in the future we intend to build a casita and tap into Herb's seedy underbelly. But, why can't we use these cute little lawn ornaments and actually house the utilities in the marker? Like a little utility box bunny we can plug things into. This practice would definitely improve my landscapers' mood.

During home building, it would not be hard to mark the utility lines and provide the homeowner the option to get their own Herb - and have an outlet in the back of his head with a protective cover? It's logical that homeowners should be aware of what utilities lie beneath their backyard and practical that they should be able to utilize it.

Let's spin some perspective. Over 700,000 underground utility lines are <u>struck</u> per year. Hitting one utility can cost hundreds of thousands of dollars and insurance usually doesn't cover that. Remember, you can also DIE. Since you struck the utility line, you get to pay fines levied by the utility company to the tune of $10,000 per hour for loss of service. Now, if you happen to shut down a hospital or factory--you can tack on the bonus of paying for their losses as well.

It doesn't make any sense. It is much easier for home builders to mark the lines, homeowners to put a bunny on it, and everyone is situationally aware and gets to use it. In discussing marking lines, the question has been posed if outhouses are on the comeback list and if they aren't, could they be?

Outhouses Are Back In Style?

You can unclench, I wouldn't say outhouses we know and despise at carnivals and concerts are floating on the upper crust of backyard must-haves. Can I get an Amen? But, I have been at several day functions in residential districts where it would have been nice to have another option. As a woman, I believe every member of the household should have their own bathroom but was out-voted.

This section is not referring to beautifully creative backyard showers near the pool. They are lovely. What I am referring to is an honest to goodness bathroom with a fully functioning toilet that is outdoors. Equipping the outdoors with a shower and sink is childsplay. The main focus is the toilet, right? That's our challenge.

Luckily, outhouses are now referred to as off-grid toilets. There are some real perks to installing one and surprisingly, several choices. Note of caution: Even if you are off-grid, some states require compost toilet regulations to be followed. Step 1 is to check with your city ordinances.

HomeBioGas: This retailer offers a Bio-Toilet Kit that doesn't tap into any sewer lines, so no city ordinances or neighbors being aware of your daily cycles. This toilet turns your waste into resources. It can service a family of 6, supply 2 hours of gas a day to cook with and has a mulch basin for your garden. If you spent the $1,600 for this toilet, you get a free Biogas stove.

Composting Toilets: No water required here. The toilet turns your waste into compost just like it says. What it doesn't say is that human waste can take up to two years to make the magic happen. If you are considering one of these toilets, make sure your game is long-term.

Incinerating Toilets: Incineration toilets burn human waste at high temperatures. A family of four can use it and at the end of the week will have one or two cups full of ash.

There are several pros and cons that come with each kind of toilet. It can lower the costs in your home too if you decide to go outdoors more than in. But, the one thing people have found that doing your business outdoors on a regular basis may mess with your <u>psyche</u>. Say what? I was shocked too. I thought the largest hurdle would be an ice cold seat during the winter causing a stunned butt. Nope.

It seems we are accustomed to seeing the water in the bowl. We are familiar with the sounds. We are calmed by the swirl of the water as the ugly is whisked away. These motions cleanse our psychological palette. There may be a tingling of uncomfortableness when trying a waterless system outdoors.

People are not used to being this aware of their release, or other people's. If you own an RV, you understand. There is a learning curve and period of adjustment as you are more involved in seeing things you are not accustomed to. Let's change the subject, we need to talk about the geese.

People Who Dress Geese

I grew up in the Midwest. We had a few strange customs over the years. Such as:

- Jackalope
- Cinnamon Rolls & Chilli
- Runzas
- Cow Tipping & Cow Chip Throwing Festival
- Duct Tape Festival
- Testicle Festival (that's deep fried turkey tesicles to be clear, let's not be weird)
- Beer butt chicken and cornflake chicken

But the most disturbing custom was dressing geese. Every day on my way to school, I would be accosted by gaggles of bikini lawn geese. I know from personal experience that geese are the devil. They are not friendly, they are angry, and they are best dressed in some orange sauce on a plate.

The trend started in the Midwest in the <u>1980s</u> and came into full bloom in the 1990s. These 65 lb. geese were wearing better clothing than I owned, and changed lovingly by owners up to 3 times per day. OK, I may have some unresolved issues. You could find them peppered across Midwest porches and front lawns, mocking me.

Geese were supposedly a thing of value from the <u>past</u> and not the demon spawn I see them as. Geese were alarms for pioneers against predatory animals. They still harbor that territorial aggression today. They also eat insects that destroy crops. Geese were good eating and used for quilts, bedding, and pillows. The purposefulness of the goose translated into a symbol of good luck and survival.

The geese were so beloved that when the July of '94 great goose-napping happened, it made front page news in the Akron Beacon-Journal. Bill the goose was kidnapped in his bikini and taken to Mount Rushmore where he sent the owner a postcard.

The paper continued its coverage of Bill's kidnapping and the editor of the paper stepped in to write an article pleading for the bird's safe return. Ummmmm, that's just wrong in too many ways. After the summer, the goose made it home and was reunited with the owner who gleefully laughed all the way through the follow-up interview. Just wow!

I was happy to see this trend fade, or so I thought. Meet Gertie goose which graced the pages as a featured story in the <u>Gazette</u>, November 2020.

The goose was dressed as a reporter on the day of the story (sigh). The boredom of COVID strikes again and people are getting sick with cabin fever. OK, so it's not really hurting anything, but it's not really helping either. See goose: <u>http://lindaksienkiewicz.com/another-goose-in-clothes-spotted/#:~:text=The%20lawn%20goose%20first%20appeared,the%20ornamental%20lawn%20goose%20family</u>.

Last Smack On The Backyard Booty

Backyard relevance has become a question of purpose and enjoyment. Americans are utilizing the space, even before COVID, but did take on a huge boom during COVID as people sought relief from being cooped up.

Backyards are fast becoming the ideal place to socialize. They contribute to our health and mental well-being. Roles have changed and home builders should pay attention to the fluidity of changing times and how easily some of the issues can be resolved. This saves everyone time and money.

CHAPTER 12

GTFO: Setbacks, Restrictions & Vertical Space

Thousands of years ago, the Indus Valley Civilization established developed cities with sophisticated planning organized according to caste, trade, and public works with functioning waste systems. Every civilization that came after aspired to perfect these basic ideals of organization and access.

Density in population requires planning to prevent chaos, and with any government and cityscape, there will be a mechanism for urban planning as a tool of survival. Survival is a team sport in the urban world. Land was a coveted commodity in America's transition from flight to fancy. Expeditions and pioneers pushed the limits of exploration for lands, even to the extent of proving the world wasn't flat.

Wars were fought with other countries and individuals who tried to claim land. Native Americans were nearly wiped out to make room for people who demanded land. People would go through personal peril to carve out a piece for themselves and build their legacy. The Oklahoma land rush was a brutal display of the risks and rewards of open land up for grabs.

Now that the frontier days are over and the land has been parceled out, do you know how much land is really yours and your rights to it? How is it that there are restrictions to what you own above, below and within your property? How is it that property lines were etched out, and public works were developed with setbacks and restrictions on our newly acquired land?

A History Of Urban Planning

The powers that be realized some type of orderly design and regulation is required to utilize space effectively for an organized, functioning city. To achieve a sophisticated society with access to public works, city <u>planners</u> would need to incorporate the knowledge of:

- Engineers
- Architects
- Social Concerns
- Political Concerns

These considerations were vital to benefit cities form, function, and accountability for social impacts of the policies implemented. City planning would require public participation and therefore warranted a specific office and discipline to develop open land and the renovation of current land use. Urban Planning was born.

Previously, towns and cities were built like small villages with a wall around it. Cities would expand, the wall would grow outward. Expansion led to poor health and conditions without a system in place to extend services to new parts of a city.

A social movement for urban reform was established in the 19th century due to the disorder and less than desirable conditions. People demanded and deserved adequate sanitation and access to amenities. Great Britain paved the way with the first academic urban planning program in Liverpool in 1909. America followed and instituted its program at Harvard in 1924. This post-doctorate study covered:

- Physical and social characteristics of an ideal city
- Possibilities on achieving change with the city's goals
- Communication and the consensus of the population
- Role of citizens, public officials, and private investors
- Quantitative analysis of data for decision making

- Environmental policies and transportation planning
- Community economic development

There were many moving parts in planning new cities. There were also specific challenges of repurposing cities already well-established while simultaneously attempting to obtain community support and participation.

It was during the Industrial Revolution (remember Central Park, suburbs, all being developed during this time) that urban planners recognized industries encroaching on residences. The answer was to create zoning regulations to separate business, recreation, and residential districts.

To take this further, Urban Planning developed rules for how tall buildings could be built and specific configurations to suburban development. Government dictated how the streets should be laid out to fit within the city planning designs so all occupants would have access to organized public works.

This is a gross oversimplification of all the moving parts that occurred for an Urban Planning Department, but it does provide the groundwork for further discussion. The Mayor and Council have final decision-making power in cities. A body of commission planners are appointed to hold the primary responsibility for urban planning, and the population at large guides these government bodies. If we are lucky, they listen.

The force of public opinion holds sway in how communities develop, which will be essential to know later. Private development proposals for new communities and redevelopment planning are presented to committees and commissioners for development based on the public's demands.

The names of the urban development planning departments may change across states, but in some form, the Mayor and an appointed council of patrons from the business community act as the board of directors and are the authority of urban planning.

Planning took a new turn at the beginning of the 20th-century with new urbanism that softened the separation of business and residential districts. The modern philosophy brought home, work, and shopping within close proximity of each other. The result is strip shopping centers near residential areas and sometimes within the community itself, often in the form of 7-11s or Starbucks on every corner. The other thing new urbanism promotes is mixed types of housing.

In recent years, sustainable development, which was advocated by the United Nations in 1987, is something that the public is rallying behind but has trouble actually implementing. Sustainable development dictates that:

"...development meets the needs of the present without compromising the ability of future generations to meet their own needs..."

The population has different views of what sustainable development should be, and the analysis of current resources is less than adequate to determine sustainability for any particular amount of time. For example, money is spent on 6 years worth of litigation regarding planting vegetables in a front yard rather than 6 years of progress towards hydroponics, 3D printing, or several other areas to improve sustainability and better land usage. This is insanity.

A Word About Property Lines

Now that we have laid the groundwork let's look at property lines. In the technology age, you can easily visit your County Assessor online and pull up your deed and the details of your home. You can see the property outline, the latitude and longitude - hell, you can even pull up an aerial view. The pool in my backyard looks like a huge penis from the air. Well-played pool guys, well-played.

Your property lines were established when your neighborhood was developed courtesy of the urban planning process we just went through. A surveyor wrote the legal descriptions for your lot, your property's measurements, and location on the plat map.

Plat maps are the outline for your entire community with the property lines carved out, resembling a massive jigsaw puzzle. Each property has a parcel number. The parcel number provides the location and identification number of your lot. These work as 'fingerprints' for your house - no two are the same.

Surveyors can help you find your property lines and play a vital role in developing new land or the redevelopment of established communities. Some cities require surveyors to verify any improvements to be done on the land, such as swimming pools or sheds, to ensure they are within the legal boundaries and meet city ordinance requirements. They obviously don't check the pool plans for indecent exposure by air, epic fail. Now, this is all well and good for walking around on the property itself, but do you think you own all of the airspace above your house? That is a hard no.

Vertical Space Property Line

As drones become more prevalent snooping into our backyards as we are privately sunbathing, you often wonder if you can shoot them down because technically, they are trespassing. Well, yes and no, depending how low the drone is flying.

The space above your land can be enjoyed 'reasonably.' Zoning laws and state statutes will restrict the heights of buildings to stop you from having access to that airspace. You can enjoy your airspace and even give others an easement to rent your <u>airspace</u> from you (utility or cellular companies can rent it for towers), but how much space is yours?

In 1946, the Supreme Court ruled the land owner could enjoy "at least as much of the space above the ground as he can occupy or use in connection with the land" but did acknowledge that the sky was becoming a public highway. The case was in reference to a plane flying 83 feet over a farmer's land and scaring his chickens. This was a problem because the chickens would panic which resulted in them running into walls and killing themselves. The farmer sued.

lthough the Supreme Court did not say how high the enjoyment was, the federal government provided the definition for us; the area 500 feet above your building is considered navigable airspace. Remember our drone? If he is flying 500 feet above the buildable surface, we cannot shoot it down, that is navigable airspace and belongs to the FAA.

The only time an aircraft can operate closer than 500 feet is in case of emergency or if it is necessary for take-off or landing. So, the answer is, the amount of vertical space you own on your lot is from the ground upward to 499 feet above the structure (360 feet above in rural areas). The Supreme Court hasn't officially accepted the mandate, but they do use it for a guideline in trespassing cases.

Recently, the federal government is entertaining the idea of lowering the navigable airspace to below 500 feet for surveillance drones. Local governments are up in arms with this new proposal due to the popularity and accessibility of surveillance drones in public hands, especially paparazzi.

What About The Space Below?

The simple answer, from the soil to hell. In no way can you expect a simple answer when the government is involved. Make friends with hints and ambiguity. If the city wanted to build a subway underneath your land, they would have to get an easement from you. However, there are instances where they don't need your permission.

The complex answer, mineral laws. Mineral laws are far more complicated and way above my paygrade. If you find oil, gas, or some other natural element, there are additional laws about who has rights to them.

Mineral rights are often sold separate from property rights. Another exclusion is if you dig and come across Indian Burial Land, you will need to report it. If you are going to dig on your property, it is advised you contact the city for any pipes under the ground. We have already divulged you would be responsible to pay should you break them. There are laws to restrict how low you can dig on your land and what resources you can extract.

When in doubt, check it out.

Property Setbacks & Restrictions

We previously covered how setbacks came to be and how they prevent land owners from building too close to the street or one another. Setbacks remain in effect until challenged or changed by law or other actions of the local government.

If you don't like the restriction, you can petition the local government for variances; however, that is usually only granted if you are suffering an extreme hardship. The ambiguity of what is extreme makes litigation over setbacks a common thing. Setbacks and restrictions were initially designed to evolve as communities changed over time. Some ordinances are so out of date that if someone were to follow them, they could create a commotion. Such as:

- <u>Williamsburg</u> is a posh neighborhood. However, according to the ordinance, you can have cattle and swine in your backyard as long as they are secured with a fence. If you want to get your neighbors attention there, you are free to purchase a pig and watch the social unrest as they can't legally do anything about it until the ordinance changes.
- In New York, you can keep chickens inside your home, just not outdoors. You also can't perform a puppet show from your window.
- In Ohio, you can't have five women living under the same roof. In Tennessee, it's eight.
- In Ohio, you can't have a slot machine in an outhouse.
- In Maryland, it is illegal to grow thistles in your yard.
- In Pennsylvania, it is illegal to hide dirt or dust with rugs.

What I am getting at is there are a lot of restrictions on the books that are not relevant. Not surprisingly, there is a lack of guidelines for what is relevant. I will bring up the 6-year lawsuit again; I just can't let it go.

Where Is The Community Relevance Committee

Let's break down the average cost of a lawsuit. You have the attorney $250-$550 an hour and filing fees, travel fees, discovery costs, court costs, on and on. This price is going to vary depending on where you live and the appeals process. Let's just make it super easy and low ball it at $3,000 per month - we can agree that a six-year lawsuit averaged way more than this, for both sides - the gardener woman vs. the city government.

12 months x 6 years = 72 months

72 months x $3,000 = $216,000

$216,000 x 2 for plaintiff and defendant = $432,000

Over tomatoes. I have made up new cuss words that would make a sailor blush over this. That's not even counting what would have had to be paid in restitution, and since the government lost the case, the taxpayers are paying this. I'm livid because I'm a taxpayer. This is only one case.

Setback litigations stemming from outdated principles wastes taxpayers' money every single year. Then, they make the laws so hard to modify that litigation is the answer for change. The perpetual cycle of bullshit renders me speechless at times. We are drifting away from the core principles of urban planning.

According to Glassdoor, urban planners make between $43,000 - $73,000 per year, depending on where they live. They have the education, experience, and skills; what they lack is the community's guidance and a model of change for outdated ordinances; including the ability to overrule and object to entertaining $432,000 6-year long lawsuits.

Why Not A Committee?

Within every zone of a city are great minds, a highly untapped resource. You have already rolled your eyes at the word 'committee' but just hear me out. What if:

- Urban planning representative
- Homebuilders/Developer representative
- Environmental Policy representative
- And 2 homeowner representatives

Worked part-time earning an additional $30,000 salary (that's $150,000 compared to the $432,000- its chump change) were to streamline the process and save the communities money while simultaneously rolling out irrelevant ordinances with a priority on ordinances and setback lawsuits that were currently in play as a mediation strategy.

This group could implement change where it is needed to renovate older developed areas and ensure that new areas were developed with sustainable features that had wiggle room for future generations. It would also allow for a convenient process for homeowners to apply for a variance without threatening lawsuits every time an outdated change was necessary. I'm not saying that lawsuits would not happen; I am saying that with a thoughtful, vested interest in the community, lawsuits would be lessened, and reason would triumph.

Homeowner Association Boards are committees that enforce city ordinances and self-police while taking the city's cost of maintaining their streets and sidewalks, among other things. They act as small governments within communities. For free. This is kind of the same principle except paid.

This Guidance Committee should be empowered to amend city ordinances and grant variances and mediate disputes and have input on new and renovated developments. Does it sound like urban planning, yes. But with one key difference, a streamlined process.

This experiment would rid the urban planning department of some of the hurdles presented in implementing sustainability by working with the public and evaluating current ordinance relevance instead of just enforcing it because it's on the books. This entity could work directly with the American Planning Association to maintain the focus of development that we have lost. Ideally, we all would learn a great deal to progress.

Public Pressure: I Mean ... Encouragement

The most remarkable changes come when there is public unrest and organization to change it. Better home development and design are well within our reach; all we need to do is be involved in making better decisions. Joining the APA is an excellent first step; convincing the city planning department with petitioning is another. Another would be to stop making confusing laws. One of the biggest laws that confuse homeowners is the ADA section.

Not All Houses Need To Be ADA

<u>FACTS</u>: The American With Disabilities Act (ADA) ***does not*** cover <u>privately</u> owned residences or individually owned or leased housing in the private sector. Only when a *public* facility is in a private sector does that public facility fall under ADA scrutiny, and it is just that facility, *not* the entire private residence.

§ 36.207 Places of public accommodation located in private residences.

- (a) When a place of public <u>accommodation</u> is located in a private residence, the portion of the residence used exclusively as a residence is not covered by this part, but that portion used exclusively in the operation of the place of public accommodation or that portion used both for the place of public accommodation and for residential purposes is covered by this part.

- (b) The portion of the residence covered under paragraph (a) of this section extends to those elements used to enter the place of public accommodation, including the homeowner's front sidewalk, if any, the door or entryway, and hallways; and those portions of the residence, interior or exterior, available to or used by customers or clients, including restrooms.

There are misconceptions about how this law works; it does not work the way you think it does, stop it.

CHAPTER 13

Rodents Infest Houses On The Ground

Rodents cause structural damage to your home, and more than that, they are scary! My suggestion for best practice on avoiding rodents is to fortify the house with a moat or burn it down to vanquish the problem. Needless to say, my suggestions are met with rolled eyes and a call to the pest control company who happily comes and fixes the problem temporarily.

Let me clarify, the fix is just for mice and insects. Pigeons roost in your roof, and their droppings saturate your ceiling and weaken it, causing leaks resembling tropical waterfalls during a rainstorm. Waterfall pigeon sludge damages your inside furnishings. If you have attracted pigeons, you will find yourself frantically swapping garbage bins and buckets under a monsoon, praying that a structural avalanche won't happen by the time you can fix the problem.

Budgeting for these types of events usually isn't in the immediate forecast for the average homeowner because things come up, like shoe sales, taking priority over saving for damages created by pests. How much these damages and pest maintenance costs vary from a few hundred to a few thousand dollars.

Don't think you require some type of pest control after seeing one mouse? It's only one, right? Fun fact, a female mouse has 5 to 10 litters of 5-6 young at a time that reproduce in 30 days. So, 30 days later, that litter will breed and become 25-60, in a year 300-720 mice are sprung from that one little mouse. Cockroaches clock in at about 18,000 a year! Ew. My moat isn't looking too shabby now, is it?

Pest Control Companies

A one-time visit from the pest <u>control</u> company costs more upfront because they need to find nests, entry points, assess the situation to see what kind of infestation you have, etc. The initial visit can be about $180 and treatment anywhere from $300-$550 due to the extensive investigation and work.

Periodic treatments via a contract are better at controlling infestations and cost around $100-$300 quarterly depending on the size and location of your house. Some companies will offer a freebie if an infestation is found between visits.

Pet Exclusion: Sealing Up Your House

Preventative maintenance is seldom enough to keep the rodents at bay. There are a few extra <u>steps</u> that you can take to avoid the rodent invasion. To properly seal up the house from unwanted guests, you need to know the entry points where they can get in.

The Foundation & Corner Posts

Entry starts with your foundation. It makes sense the closer your foundation is to the ground the more highly susceptible your home is to rodent penetration. Foundations crack, leaving an open door.

Corner posts and J channels on the exterior of your home are hollow and serve as an open invitation to rodents who easily shimmy up the side of your house and go through the hollow posts. This is how rodents get inside your walls.

One way to seal these areas is with caulk and copper wire mesh. Copper wire works better than steel wire because the texture of copper wire gets stuck in rodents' teeth, making it difficult for them to chew through. Copper prevents them from moving, acting as an adequate deterrent. Putting this mix in any hole you find and around windows and corners will help keep pests out of your home.

Garages & Cellars

Make sure your garage door closes snugly with no gaps and is not uneven. Also, leaving your garage door open for extended periods is like a torch in the dark, attracting rodents to the flame, especially if your garage is disorganized and cluttered with plenty of hiding spots. Break these bad habits now to discourage the little pests.

You can fill holes you see, including cracks in the cement, with the caulk and copper wire mixture to solidify the preventative measures. Many garages are not insulated or finished, so the weak condition is ripe for rodents to take up lodging.

If you have cellar doors, rats and mice will fall through the cracks by accident or on purpose. A best practice is to seal the door gap with some heavy-duty weather stripping and fill any visible holes with the caulking mix.

Gutters & Chimneys

Rodents' superpower is the ability to climb up open shafts to make their way into your home. This is especially true in the case of gutters and chimneys. For a gutter, install mesh on the opening such as chicken wire or copper mesh at the downspout opening.

You will need to mark it on your calendar to remove the mesh once a week to let debris flow out and not clog up the gutters. The chimney is a bit trickier but not unsolvable. If rodents gain access to the roof, they expertly crawl right down the heart of it and enter your house.

You can make it an obstacle for them by installing 12-inch wide sheet metal at the chimney's base. Their little feet won't grip because it is too slippery, and they won't be able to make their way into your chimney.

Pest Prevention By Design

In the interest of a greener world, pet exclusion tactics are finally making their way into structural design in housing. The theory is to make the home sealed off and unappealing to rodents because it is cheaper and safer than applying chemicals for a temporary solution.

Pet Exclusion is homebuilding that discourages pests from taking up residence in the first place and is a permanent year-round solution. Chris Geiger, Ph.D. (San Francisco Department of the Environment) and Caroline Cox, MS (Center for Environmental Health) authored <u>Pest Prevention By Design</u>, which was co-signed by the International Code Council.

The US Centers for Disease Control provided a grant for the research, development, and guidelines of implementing pest exclusion into structures. They documented what materials should be used in specific zones to combat infestations common within those areas. Most of the US looks to the ICC for sustainable design, construction, and development codes.

Working under an extensive list of advisors, the guidelines illustrate the future of pest strategy by capitalizing on material uses and locations. Their goal:

To create a set of authoritative, peer-reviewed guidelines for designing and building pests out of buildings.

These guidelines take home developers through the entire process, from foundation to roof and even landscaping. The manuscript also contains a resolution for all sorts of insects, mammals, and birds. Would it be a good idea to move from guidelines to adopting them into a city ordinance? (HINT) That remains to be seen.

For now, builders have the option to utilize this information or toss it to the side. If you are building a home, you may want to provide these guidelines to your builder; if you are not, maybe a committee meeting is in order.

CHAPTER 14

Garages: Attached or Detached

Over 82 <u>million</u> American homes have a garage. If you couple that with the fact that over 71% of homeowners use their garage entrance as the front door, it is made clear the garage is deserving of our attention in this manifesto.

When garages arrived on the scene in the 1920s, it was nothing short of birth by fire. Only six years later, the automatic garage opener was invented. Insane, right? That is before several conveniences of the modern home we discussed in previous chapters came into existence! Even before that, in <u>1908</u>, Sears & Roebuck had a portable garage you could take anywhere.

Garages have housed start-up companies, fantastic inventions, legendary bands, and yes, even your car. Plenty of good has come out of the garage, including:

- Apple
- Amazon
- Disney
- Google
- Harley-Davidson
- The Beatles
- The Ramones

- Nirvana
- The Who
- The Kinks

The garage culture is historically significant, and 52% of homeowners want a garage their neighbors envy. Go forth and create your office, man cave, entertainment room, or game room, but close up shop gents, put the cars where they belong. After all, that is the reason why garages were invented in the first place.

The History Of Garages

With the invention of the automobile came the need to store the vehicle to protect it from the elements. At first, people used their carriage houses previously used for buggies. Those that didn't have a carriage house could rent a carriage house at a nearby farm or home for $15-$20 a month. Gotta love the entrepreneurial spirit in America.

The carriage houses were heated and clean, and the owner made sure to maintain the space for their renters properly. However, animals were also housed in the carriage house and, well, have you ever tried to get cat urine smell out of a leather jacket? Simultaneously, cars started getting more affordable, and it was quickly noticed we needed another way to store vehicles.

Enter the garage or motor house. What started as sheds and portable units evolved at neck-breaking speed into full-fledged garages. At first, the sheds had large swinging doors which took considerable time and effort to deal with. Sliding doors were invented in the 1920s, and the overhead garage door was roughly a year later. The electric garage door opener followed in 1926 and was a game-changer.

Homeowners started asking about garages when they were looking to buy a new home, and having a garage was a deciding factor in purchasing the home. By the 1940s, garages were incorporated into home design rather than being standoffish. By the 1960s, most families had two cars leading to two-car garages. Garage space increased; taking up approximately 45% square footage of the average home.

Attached Garage Evolution

With technological advancements in garage flooring and heating, garages have become multipurpose. With garages taking up 45% plus of house space, they should be. They should also adequately house your car. If you need an additional room, build an additional room. Great examples at: https://www.dreamcoatflooring.com/ and https://www.mancaveknowhow.com/

The ability for garage greatness is there; but why is it that:

- 50% of homeowners plan to reorganize their garage so they can enjoy it more
- 20% say they have difficulty parking in the garage
- 89% of garage owners want to improve their garage space

Popular opinion shows more planning needs to be focused on the garage to optimize function when you purchase your home.

Garage MakeOver

Garages are usually cemented floors with quick, unfinished walls and no storage space to think of. The garage often becomes a free for all of the items on one side with a small space for your car marked by the stains. What most people don't realize is that garages can play a large role in energy efficiency for your home.

Garage remodels cost as much as $10,000, but luckily, a lot can be done as DIY projects to cut costs considerably. Remodeling affords the benefit of saving on energy and increasing the value of your home instantly. Over 82% of realtors indicate a remodeled garage increases the selling price, value, and will be a contributing factor to the sale.

Energy Efficiency

Garages are usually the most uninsulated room in your house with a direct pathway to the elements. The air temperature in your garage will cross over to the attached rooms beside, above, or below and push your home's <u>utilities</u> to work harder to cool or heat your home.

The garage should be a finished room just like any other room in your home. Garages are an extension of your home and affect how your home operates in both organization and energy. Most garages built today are not insulated; it is an easy fix with:

- Rolling insulation between joists
- Blowing insulation through a small hole in the drywall

Generally, this is only about $1,000 for a two-car garage. Additionally, adding caulking to wall joints and weatherstripping will help seal in the insulation. Finally, you can purchase insulated garage doors for under $1,000 as well. These small investments would pay for themselves in utility costs.

For those of you that love working in your garage, ditch the heaters and stand-alone air conditioners for solar panels. Passive solar panels are available for about $50 for heating, and you simply cover them when you don't need the heat. Another useful addition is LED lighting, which saves about 80% of energy costs and lasts longer.

Garage Flooring

Cement floors crack due to expansion in changing temperatures, leading to an influx in heating and cooling. Not to mention, cement allows for unsightly marks on the garage floors because it does not resist hot tire marks or oil, which are difficult to clean.

Epoxy floors or polyaspartic flooring like <u>Floortex</u> provide the best protection and acts as a barrier between walls and flooring to maintain the insulation. Upgrading your garage floor is typically a one day DIY project that pays off huge. Some of the benefits of Floortex are:

- Doesn't yellow
- Impact-resistant
- Chemical resistant (oil, gas, tires, etc.)
- Waterproof

The right garage floor enhances the energy-efficiency of your entire home.

Organization In The Garage

You may think your cluttered garage won't impact the energy efficiency of your home, but it does. Piles attract rodents and pests that eat your freshly installed insulation and defeat the purpose.

Storage units will keep items organized and locked away from pests; they will help regulate your garage's temperature, which helps maintain the temperature in your home. However, if you take the advice of previous chapters in optimizing your home space, you won't need a storage unit.

Old Appliances

Running a fridge or freezer in your garage built before 1990 and doesn't have the Energy Star is costing you between $250-$300 extra a year and is a drain on the resources.

Homebuilders Need To Finish The Garage

Garages need to be more than an afterthought when building homes. You see all of the strong declarations by home builders of energy-efficient smart homes, but then they leave 45% unfinished (the garage) effectively unraveling everything accomplished.

At a bare minimum, insulation and flooring need to be considered, so homeowners are not forced into building efficiency ass-backward. Popular opinion (and science) demands it.

Detached Beautimous

Having a detached garage means you don't need to concern yourself with heating and cooling expenses or well-padded insulation, unless you frequently tinker in the garage. Separated garages don't have to be an eyesore that doesn't match the house. Rather, separated garages are a distinction from a living dwelling and add stature and elegance to a home.

The Good, Bad & Ugly of Outdoor Structures

The screams for outdoor living have grown more aggressive since the age of COVID. She-sheds, office huts, gazebos, workshops, and various other closet cubicles are being assembled across the country in backyards everywhere.

Let it be known--just because you can, doesn't always mean you should. Just because outdoor living is an attractive amenity, does not mean we put the breaks on progress and revert to trending stylish outhouses all over the internet. Yes, I am aware there is an outhouse section in this book and I am walking contradiction - one of my more endearing qualities.

When it comes to outdoor structures, functionality and aesthetics need to come into play. After all, living outdoors requires you to experience the outdoors. Building the 'indoors' in the 'outdoors' defeats the purpose. We have toured a bit of the good, bad, and ugly and put them here as either a cautionary tale, or inspiration--appropriately labeled with our Yay or Nay.

Gazebos - YAY

Gazebos add value to your home and according to 51% of <u>buyers</u>, gazebos are an attractive quality in a home outranking curb appeal and open floor plans. Gazebos have been the centerpiece for the greatest love scenes of all-time (Sound of Music). The nostalgic appeal is desirable for weddings and romance.

It was not uncommon for smaller cities to have a large gazebo in the center of town for celebrations, gatherings, and <u>bandstands</u> (GroundHog Day). The charm is undeniable.

Gazebos are timeless epitomes of style, luxury, and sophistication. Interacting with the outdoors while lounging in a gazebo reeks of 'the good life' and the best of both worlds as you taste both indoor and outdoor elements.

You can bet your biscuits those damnable Romans had everything to do with gazebos. Both Greeks and Romans featured luscious gardens dancing around marble gazebos serving as temples to gods and goddesses. They also enjoyed gazebos in their home gardens as a place to relax and converse with friends.

During the medieval and renaissance period, churches and the wealthy cornered the market on elaborately designed gazebos surrounded by a moat of rich gardens. Gazebos would be used for meditation and shrines. Lords and ladies would erect gazebos far from the home so the guests could walk through the estate and admire the gardens leisurely before gathering at the gazebo to rest and refresh.

Tea houses in Asia are forms of gazebos that have been popular in China and Japan for centuries. Tea houses are used for rest, meditation, reflection and gatherings. With such an established, regal history, gazebos weigh in as a yay.

Building a gazebo isn't overly expensive and there are <u>kits</u> that can assist the DIY enthusiasts. On average, building a gazebo costs around $6,500 and the kits are between $1,500 and $7,000. It all depends on your style.

Some people agonize for months on whether they want a pergola or a gazebo. The only difference is the roof. Pergolas let light in with a slatted roof while gazebos offer complete shade. Tomatoe, tomato.

Storage Sheds or She Sheds - That's A Hard Nay

This one is right up there with cars on blocks. Why? Storage sheds are notorious targets for robbers. That sucks too because being 'burgled' sounds absolutely delightful - it's such a cute word. I know that we advocate sheds early in this book, but the suggestion is secondary to planning your home so you don't need them. The reality is sheds store valuable, useful things worth money; however, they are not at all secure and therefore, are easy prey.

Sheds are notorious for becoming eyesores and the bane of your, and a Homeowner Association's, existence because every Karen comes out of the woodwork to complain about them. Sheds are a pest playground for both hostile Karens and small rodents.

If you are looking for a studio, office, workshop, or storage - the best form for function would actually be a repurposed pool house villa. Just because you don't have a pool doesn't mean you can't use a pool house to create the space you need for yourself or space you can rent out or sequester visiting family members.

These structures are prefab, customizable, and a few thousand more than you would pay for some storage sheds. They are by far more durable, spacious, secure, versatile, and add value to the home, not an eyesore or welcome wagon for pest infestation or burglary. The prestige that comes with saying you have a pool house vs. a storage shed are indisputable.

Building Restriction Lines - The Ugly

Rules on what you can build on your property require a heavy review of vocabulary before we can tackle the subject matter. So, with great annoyance, I present building restrictions - The Ugly.

What do governments, politics, and my ex-husband have in common? The obvious guess is he's a politician. Nope, they are all narcissistic. But, in this case, narcissism serves a purpose in the form of building codes preventing catastrophic consequences.

Ancient civilizations had building codes -- written ones (we found them). Hammurabi formed the <u>Babylonian</u> Empire with them in 2000 BC and it is firmly believed that codes existed 4,000 years prior. Poor building practices can be the death of a sustainable, functioning community. In the states, building codes showed up in about 1625 to raise roofing standards (see what I did there). Fun facts:

1630 Boston outlawed wooden chimneys

1770 George Washington imposed height limitations on wood framed buildings

1788 building codes were imposed regarding fire hazards in Salem (witch trials)

1862 exit requirements became prominent

1865 New Orleans started the inspection of public places trend

There was a Roman architect from the first century named Marcos Vitruvius. If there was ever a great name for a frozen specialty drink at a bar -- that's it. Anyway, he is referred to as the great Roman architect and achieved creating elevators and siege engines to name a few inventions.

Vitruvius wrote a remarkable ten-volume library of building technology which is the basis of several concepts used today on:

- Building structures
- City planning
- Building materials
- Acoustics
- Timekeeping, water clocks & sundials
- Pumps
- Astronomy
- Music
- Arts
- Medicine; and
- Contract Law

The man was brilliant and tinkered with everything adeptly spinning copper into gold. George Washington and Thomas Jefferson paid close attention to these mechanics as well as plots and maps and molded the clay that is Roman architecture and city planning into the shining pillar of government that it is today. The echoes of their wisdom can be heard from your backyard building restrictions.

As we discussed earlier, when you buy a home, you receive a survey plat. The plat is recorded with the county you live in and serves as a legal description of what you own. On this plat, it shows where your property lines are, where your neighbor's property line is, and where you are allowed to build. If you are going to put a fence around your yard, this is especially helpful. In review, to amend property lines and alter setbacks - see the previous chapter on setback restrictions. As we get into this, it will help to know a little vocabulary:

Building Lines - Building lines note the distance from the sides of a lot and where you can build something. There is a required amount of space that you need to leave between things, known as setbacks. The structure must 'set back' some space away from the property line. Note: If you don't do it right, the city can make you tear it down or they will do it for you at a cost. See example: https://planningdevelopment.elpasoco.com/planning-development-questions/#1516896259595-24f3e76f-233f

Easements - An easement grants someone or a group/organization the right to use your property for a specific purpose. For example, a utility company having an easement to read a meter, or run pipes underground. You cannot build things that will interfere with an easement. This includes if your neighbor has to walk up your driveway to get into his backyard. You can't block or restrict access.

Building Codes - Building codes are determined by the city you live in, so they can be different from place to place.

Every reason above is why you want to work with a contractor that you researched extensively before hiring. If things are done wrong, it will cost you to tear it down and you may not be able to complete the project. There is also the likely possibility of fines until it is corrected. Speaking of fines, building restrictions are not the only thing you need to worry about when building in some communities. There is a greater evil at work here called Homeowner Associations.

Homeowner Associations - The Diabolical

Like any deity with narcissistic rage, Homeowners Associations have good intentions, and can be fantastic in providing services to its members - but there can be a darker side that runs the community with a strong fist and tyrant ambitions. It depends on the Board of elected homeowners governing it.

Homeowner Associations (HOA) can be multi-hyphenated confusing because there is talk of air space that you own, exterior walls that you own but did not build, or your satellite dish may cause a ruckus, or the removal of a bush in your front yard or parking your commercial truck in your driveway may land you in an HOA hearing with complimentary HOA fines. You can even belong to 2 HOAs at the same time!

I touched on HOAs briefly, but there are a few points I didn't make earlier that need to be amplified here:

1. Review the Codes, Covenants & Restrictions (CC&Rs) **BEFORE** you decide to purchase the house. Yes, you can do that. This tells you what you can and can't do with your property. For example, painting your home neon colors is frowned upon and will get you fined until it is corrected. The HOA will either have paint swatches or you need to bring them examples. But, restrictions go much deeper than that, so read.

-   If you do not pay the HOA assessments, they can foreclose on your home whether or not you are current with your mortgage. If you have a disagreement with your HOA on park equipment repairs or anything else, do not attempt to withhold payment for HOA assessments.

You always could find out if you have a regime style HOA Board, but new board members are elected about every 2 years, so the theme can change frequently. HOA Boards will enforce some rules more than others and some not at all. It depends greatly on what the current HOA Board believes is important for the community to flourish.

In 1995, there was a movie that scarred me for life when it came to HOAs. I grew up in a small town with country roots, so my perception of the world was influenced by what I saw on TV or what I read in books. Jack Ritter from Three's Company was one of my mom's favorite actors and therefore, one of mine at the time.

He starred in a TV movie about a man who moved his family from the crime-ridden city and into the peaceful, quiet, gated community in the suburbs. The Burbs movie had come out a few years before this movie and educated me on what living in suburbia was like in all its splendor.

This specific suburbian eden was attractive to Ritter because it was violence-free and stock full of people who had their lives together and living in perfection - white picket fence and all.

The movie was called The Colony and when you aim for the perfect life, you must sacrifice civil liberties and become the beast of uniformity. There are consequences if you don't. For example, the family dog barked too much and The Colony took the dog's vocal box out. There is no where to watch it except YouTube: https://www.youtube.com/watch?v=rXBRJWF4Y-U

OK, so the movie is a bit '90s (made in 1995), but it is fun to watch and leaves an impression of the overly enthusiastic and invasive rules of HOAs. I am pleased to report I live in an HOA and although there has been, what I feel, is an overaction for driving an ATV behind my kids as they went trick or treating because I was too lazy to walk - living here has been relatively pleasant (Chants ONE OF US in my head).

My Home Is My Castle - Kinda Sorda

How is it that people can tell us what to do with our homes? I thought my home was my castle!

Well, yes and no. The old phrase of home and castle goes back to British proverbs. Your home is your place of safety and where you are supreme boss (on the inside of your home) and have the right to defend, protect, and enjoy it.

The phrase also hints that problems occurring in the home should be controlled and solved there rather than putting it to outsiders. Homes and castles are juicy with privacy and security. What it is not: Devine control over the outside of your home.

During the 17th century, a judge named Sir Edward <u>Coke</u>, over the pond in England, uttered:

"For a man's house is his castle, et domus sua cuique est tutissimum refugium (Every man's home is his safest refuge)" while presiding over a case. The case was regarding the local Sheriff bursting into homes uninvited and unannounced. The British Prime Minister George Grenville added to the sentiment in 1763:

"The poorest man may in his cottage bid defiance to all the forces of the crown. It may be frail — its roof may shake — the wind may blow through it — the storm may enter — the rain may enter — but the King of England cannot enter."

That's pretty romantic right? I'm a sucker for rebellion. But the thing is, ancient codes and city planning have been in play since the beginning of time because what you do on the outside has the potential to affect others in negative ways or deprive them of public services. For example, access to public utilities, or to their own home.

However, what you do inside your home is your business (unless it is illegal, then stop it). The homes and castles doctrine protects the indoors and not the moat. Another phrase you could compare it to is behind closed doors = secret. Or maybe, what happens in Vegas stays in Vegas.

As much as building restrictions may suck - and some may be wildly out of date as humans continue to encroach upon each other - they are there for the greater good and equal enforcement. This is comparable to the phrase - I hate everyone equally. The good thing about the inside of your home is you know what every room is...or do you?

CHAPTER 16

Siding Is A Thing?

As you know, I grew up in Nebraska. What you may not know is: Nebraska is smack dab in the middle of tornado alley. I saw every color of sky. No, I don't mean rainbows (although I saw those too). The storm skies are what I am referring to. Green is the color of tornadoes.

If you talk to anyone in the Midwest, they have had a tornado encounter. The closest one I had was when my cousin, grandparents, and myself were going to Worlds of Fun (a theme park) in Kansas City, Missouri. I was about 5-years-old and my cousin was a year younger.

In those days, there were no seatbelt laws. My cousin and I were sprawled out and sleeping in the backseat. I felt a burst of speed jolting the car forward. Speed was something quite out of the ordinary when driving with grandparents. Usually grandparents are in the fast lane traveling at 45 mph. The unusual activity coupled with seeing my grandpa's eyes locked on something in the rearview mirror and his forehead wrinkled in concern, made me sit on my knees to look out the rear window.

Not one, but THREE, small tornadoes were skipping across the highway playing tag and toying with traffic. The fun in this game is anticipating which way the tornadoes were going to turn. Cornfields lay to the left and right of the highway as the twisters bounced down the highway in the center. Another thing was down the center; me. This was not a fun way to wake up. Not a peep had come from my grandparents.

In their years of seasoned tornado-dodging, grandpa calmly pushed the pedal to the floor and didn't let up until the dancing trio of terror dissipated. He wasn't playing. A tornado had destroyed grandpa's farm before I was born and I had heard tales of pieces of straw penetrating 2 x 4s.

Tornadoes had a bit of an entourage. The entourage consists of tornado sirens, ominous clouds, thick smell of rain, calm, wind, green skies, and hail. Hail would pound us until we ran inside and away from watching the tornado skies. These little ice bullets were various in size. Some were pea-sized, others baseball-sized.

Hail damage is real. They would leave welts, damage cars, homes, and utility poles. Most homeowner insurance policies carried a hail exclusion as a force of nature; you had to pay extra for specific hail coverage. Having his house demolished by tornadoes and having to make various storm repairs over the years led my grandfather to invest in aluminum siding for his home.

Every time it hailed, the noise of hail ricocheting off the siding was deafening. In response, grandpa would turn up the TV in the basement to drown out the noise. My ears would ring for hours when all was said and done.

After the storm, grandpa would go out and put his hands in his pockets while he looked at the sky and looked at the siding with a look of contentment on his face. I never knew if it was the fact the house was still standing that pleased him, or if it was the confidence he had in the aluminum siding to make the home indestructible. We are about to find out.

Types Of Siding

Before we ask why, we should probably go into the various kinds of siding out there and what they do. According to HGTV, there are 6 best types of siding, so those are the ones we will cover. I don't know if all these different types were available at the time my grandpa built his house in the 1980s, but he still would have gone with aluminum because the man was a legend.

People add siding to their home for several reasons. The most common reasons are aesthetics and protection. Siding performs functions that paint doesn't. Such as, a resistance to water or pests. The material, depending on what you get, is fairly durable and versatile. You can even make your home look like stone or red cedar; kind of like floor tiling but for the side of your house.

Vinyl Siding

Vinyl siding is attractive because it is low-cost and easily maintained. It is the most popular choice in America. There is a wide range of colors and styles that overwhelm the plastic look of the product. Vinyl is sexy because of the various customization options.

Vinyl siding is accessible at nearly every home improvement store. The availability and cost make it appealing for DIY projects. A little time and boom - you have a completely different looking home. Manufacturers have the how-to videos of their products on YouTube. Well played, Vinyl. Well played.

Wood Siding

Wood siding is popular among comfy hideaway bungalows and cottages. Wood siding obviously doesn't retain a plastic-look and appears more wealthy and durable. It does require more maintenance than vinyl siding and it will succumb to insects and rodents. Wood siding, if maintained properly, can last 10 to 100 years.

Wood siding doesn't come in long panels like vinyl siding. It's more like shingles on the side of your house instead of your roof. This lap application is called bevel siding. Planks of wood are installed horizontally and another plank will be installed to overlap the piece below. You can also opt for shingles and shakes. Manufacturers sometimes offer fire-retardant chemicals due to wood in high-risk locales. You can expect wood siding to cost around $5-$10 a sq foot, not including painting, staining, or labor.

Brick Siding

Brick siding reminds me of the *Three Little Pigs* which is a horror story when you live in tornado alley. Brick siding is made from fired clay and comes in all shapes, sizes, and textures. You can expect to find brick siding on Colonial, Tudor, and English homes and cottages of the countryside. It is beautiful.

The bad news is that water can penetrate brick veneers. The good news is that you can install a membrane between the wood and brick to protect the home. Brick siding will outlive you if properly maintained and installed. Installation is labor intensive. Both the durability and installation time make it a more expensive option. You can expect to pay $6-$15 a square foot.

Fiber-Cement Siding

Fiber-cement siding looks like stone or wood but isn't as expensive as the real thing. It's like faux-stone. This type of siding is attractive because it is low maintenance, non-flammable, and resists termites. There are a ton of different styles, textures, and finishes to choose from.

Although fiber-cement siding is impressive in resisting certain things, it is not resistant to moisture. Asbestos is a concern In homes that used this type of siding before the late 1980s. You can expect the siding to last for about 25 to 50 years which will bring your price tag to about $6-$12 per sq foot; not including trim.

Stucco Siding

Living in the west, I am not a fan of stucco. However, it makes the honorable mention for being the most popular beige element of desert landscaping (#blending). Stucco is a sand, cement, lime, and water mixture that is sprayed over a waterproof barrier and galvanized-metal screening over a layer of wood walls. It kind of looks like popcorn going over chicken wire. It is rough and sharp as the dickens.

Stucco is rigid and requires professional installation otherwise it cracks. We are told that if stucco siding is properly installed it can last the lifetime of the home. I am not buying that for a minute. Stucco chips on its rough edges and every time I walk by it, I have to suppress my desire to take a sandpaper tool to it for snagging on nearly every sweater that I own. If your depth perception is better than mine, which is a high probability, this may be the siding for you.

Stone and Stone-Veneer Siding

This is probably my all time favorite siding. I think it appeals to my deep-seated need to feel like a princess. The natural beauty of this siding is undeniable. Stone is durable and aesthetically pleasing. Granite and limestone can add all sorts of dimensions to your home's exterior. Stone is more expensive than the previous options and is a challenge to add to some homes.

This siding is still less expensive than the real thing and stone-veneer siding comes in both natural and synthetic materials. Stone siding does need to be cleaned annually. A hose works nicely along with a cursory inspection to take care of any issues. You will be pleased to know this siding will outlive you, but the cost may kill you. You can expect to pay between $10-$30 a sq foot.

Why Siding

Now that we have ventured through the *what* of siding, the next question is the *why* of siding. According to Remodeling Magazine's Cost vs. Value Report, siding does increase home value by nearly 77% of the project cost. That does say a lot, but what else?

- <u>Appearance</u> - Siding transforms your home from old to new. It is an extreme makeover and makes the home look modern and fresh. You can add trim accents for vibrant color schemes. Siding retains its color year round.

- Energy Efficiency - Today's siding installations usually include more insulation, sealing air leakage problem areas. Not only do you get an excellent rate of return on curb appeal and increased home value; you feel it in your pocketbook every month by paying less in cooling and heating costs.

- Catch Costly Problems - Some homes are high-risk for leaks, mold, and rot. Installing siding allows those problems to be fixed and shored up before becoming costly. These are also usually problems that you will not see again after installing siding.

- Low-Maintenance & No More Painting Costs - A good cleaning once a year is all that siding requires. This is much less expensive than painting each year; about $50,000 less expensive. Most siding is resistant to pests and rot, so no costly repairs. There is no cracking, peeling, or corroding.

- Element Protection - Most siding protects homes from the elements and withstands winds of 110 mph or more. Insulated siding with a foam core provides improved impact resistance because the foam is a shock absorber. It appears grandpa was right. This absorber provides protection against hail, rocks, or baseballs from the neighbor's kid.

- Insurance Premiums - Specific kinds of siding, depending where you live, can lower insurance premiums by 20%.

It is fair to say that I am sold on siding. Siding seems to be the gift that keeps on giving. Nicely done! I wonder if roofs can have the same type of impact.

CHAPTER 17

Look Up & Maintain Your Roof

Growing up, air conditioners were on roofs. At the time, I thought the practice was ridiculous. It wasn't until I moved to Nevada that I understood. Nevada is a desert. In the desert it is H-O-T. Like stepping out of your door into a hair dryer on high heat. It was during the hottest year that I was pregnant, in the dead of summer, during a heat wave. My air conditioner busted. When Nevada sends out heat warnings that means it is 120 degrees in the shade.

Let's set the scene. Heat warnings also mean air conditioners are blowing up all over the Valley. Air conditioners can not handle cooling the house to a balmy 90 degrees, much less 70, in the scorching heat. In Las Vegas, there are long waiting lists for parts during the summer. A/C units spike in price and only those with great credit can get them without a bundle of bribery and cash. The power company is forbidden from turning off the electricity when old or young members live in the home because the heat kills people. AND it was the year I discovered what copper theft was.

Air conditioning units were being stolen from the sides of homes. People were installing lockboxes around their units. Yup, putting A/C units on the roof started making a lot more sense. These were my thoughts as I was hot, 8 months pregnant and sitting on a leather couch in front of a swamp cooler that did nothing but add humidity to the heat. It was stifling and juicy at the same time. I was in a dark place and contemplated selling my unborn child for an air conditioner. This story becomes relevant later, promise.

The air conditioner did eventually get repaired, but this was not my defining moment on how important roofs were. No, that came much later in a conversation I was having with an HOA Board member about feeding Alka-Seltzer to pigeons. Pigeons in Las Vegas are not like pigeons in Nebraska.

In Nebraska, if you were a teen looking for some extra cash during the summer without really working for it, you had two choices. One, you would catch crawdads out of the ditches and sell them to bait shops, or two, you would visit farmers and ask if you could clear out a silo. Clearing out a silo meant shooting the pigeons that were roosting in the silo and eating the corn inside.

Corn-fed pigeons were fat, tasty morsels that you could sell for meat. Las Vegas pigeons eat trash. Let's just say, you really are what you eat. The pigeon population in Las Vegas is swelling and a right nuisance. In 2019, someone even tried to spruce up the strip by gluing little cowboy <u>hats</u> to pigeons' heads. It went viral on Facebook: <u>https://www.insider.com/pigeons-las-vegas-cowboy-hats-viral-video-2019-12</u>

Back to the point, pigeons are a nuisance because they nest in roofs and end up damaging them. The conversation with the HOA Board member was a result of pigeons infesting several condos and damaging the roofs causing leaks. The Board didn't want to continue to pay for the pest control and wanted a permanent solution.

He mentioned that he had read an article that Alka-Seltzer causes gas to swell the pigeon's stomach because they can't emit it, causing the pigeon to self-combust. FYI, pigeons can burp, this doesn't kill them. He also brought up the idea of rice. Dry rice expands when exposed to liquid. The idea is the pigeon eats it, expands, and again the pigeon explodes. Birds regurgitate. Rice is not the answer.

This debate in pigeon-lore took two-hours of my life that I will never get back. The Board member finally opted for pest control to clear the pigeons and for pigeon deterrents to be installed. Deterrents don't let them land. If pigeons can't land, they can't roost and will therefore move on to the next victim. Needle strips, netting, and shock tracks do nicely. Shooting them is frowned upon in Las Vegas. However, there was nearly a pigeon masacre in the great roof fall of 2017; that would be me.

Despite deterrents on my roof, pigeons found a weakness and infested an area of my roof unbeknownst to me. That is until my roof collapsed during a particularly rainy spell in the desert. This is my life mind you. No air conditioning and pregnant = heat wave. My life dictates that this would be the time for a continuous downpouring of rain IN A DESERT. I was wet, ankle deep in pigeon poop and filth because no one can fix my roof in a storm. My roof collapsed because pigeons soiled through it and the weight could not handle the pounding of rain.

That was my defining moment. You know how people used to get slimed on Nickelodeon? An army of buckets would appear and slime the victim in a sea of green. That was me but it wasn't slime. It was something more dark and sinister, an insidious goop. After cleaning the mess the best I could (Bleach is my friend), I had to set my alarm to change the buckets, pots, and trash cans every two hours. Beautiful. I learned that all <u>roofs</u> are not equal.

What Kind of Roofs Are There?

The kind of roof you have largely depends on the <u>area</u> of the US you live in. The main purpose of a roof is to protect us from the elements; and pigeon sludge. Therefore, the roof depends on the elements that you are subjected to.

The Northeast is familiar with bitter cold, snow storms, and frigid mother nature. You will find a large amount of asphalt shingles there because asphalt insulates homes and can support the weight of heavy snow.

The Southeast endures tropical storms, hurricanes and high winds on the fly and without warning. Since water surrounds the skies, metal is the roofing of choice. Metal isn't affected by humidity and won't fester algae, mold, and other related problems.

If you don't like the weather in the Midwest, you wait five minutes because it will change. The variety of weather patterns experienced there is dizzying. Large snowfalls, ominous thunderstorms, wind, and hail. Slate tiles are preferred because they don't buckle under the pressure that mother nature throws out.

The Great Plains states are attractive and isolated. There are no close neighbors or towns, so homeowners must be self-sufficient. Wood satisfies the weather and maintenance requirements for those strong, handy folks.

The Southwest is known for unrelenting sun, deserts, and HEAT. Clay tiles are popular because they provide air circulation and natural insulation. Clay reflects the overwhelming heat and naturally fits with the decor of desert dwellers.

Lastly, the Northwest is green and lush thanks to the abundance of rain. Two kinds of roofs are prevalent here. Treated asphalt to repel moisture and metal roofing because of the moisture resistance. Let's go through these popular choices, and one not listed here that deserves mention.

Asphalt Shingles - Durable, inexpensive, and easy to install makes asphalt shingles a popular choice. There are a variety of colors and styles that will hold up under several different climates. These shingles can last between 15 to 20 years. There is an option to treat them for damper conditions.

Ceramic/Clay Roofing Tiles - These tiles are fairly durable, fade-resistant, and fireproof. They also last longer than asphalt shingles - about 50 to 70 years. This feature does make them a bit more expensive. Ceramic tiles overlap each other to keep out rainwater, but are not adequate for weather that changes often because they are prone to erosion. Ceramic tiles are ceramic - so they are fragile and not great for high winds. They also can't hold the pressure of air conditioners or people walking on them.

Slate Roof Shingles - These shingles are on the wealthier side of things for several different reasons. They are natural looking, fire resistant, invulnerable to rot, easy to maintain and can last 100 years. It is beneficial to spring the bucks if you have them to do your roof one time in your life. Set it and forget it. One drawback is that these shingles are heavy. Another is that they require specialized installation because they break if stepped on which makes for difficult maintenance or gutter cleaning.

Wood Shakes & Cedar Shingles - As odd as it sounds, wood is ideal in hot and sunny climates because they resist UV damage. They can also hold their own in harsh weather conditions. The wood shingles are coated with fire-resistant treatment, so that is a plus. Wood shakes are more green-friendly than other methods listed here if you want to make an environmentally sound choice. You can expect them to last about 30 years. Cedar roofs also cut down energy expenses but are more difficult to install which makes it more expensive but you can make up for that in energy costs.

Metal Roofing - Metal shingles are attractive because of the low maintenance, light weight, and environmentally friendly aspects. Installation is challenging so you will need an expert. Metal roofing does fade but a quick repaint puts you back in the trending category.

What About Solar?

A few years ago, I was curious about solar because my utility bills are outrageous. This is when I found out that angles and roof space matter. It turns out that because my roof is odd and has several twists and turns, I could fit 8 solar panels on the roof. I thought - EIGHT hurray!!! That should take my utilities down to nothing! I was being overly optimistic. I don't do math, I do research.

The average American home needs between 21 to 34 solar panels to cover the electric bill. This means I need 369 square feet of roof space. This is easier said than done with the peaks and valleys in my roof. No wonder it is so attractive to pigeons.

Not to mention this 21 to 34 calculation is based on the US Energy Information Administration's average of 877 kilowatt hours used in the home and 280-watt solar panels. I am egregiously above average in electricity usage on my local utility bill, I know I don't fit into the 21 to 34 panel average no matter how badly I want to. So, 8 panels wasn't going to cut it.

You can use a solar calculator to find out how many panels you will need. Warning, most solar calculators do not tell you how many panels. They do tell you that your roof is a great candidate, you can receive rebates, and how much energy savings you can expect per month. They then provide you a number for a free estimate. That is when you find out about the truth of square footage on your roof. Granted, your truth may be very different from mine. Or you could figure out how many panels you need the old fashioned way.

The number of panels your home needs depends on:

- The amount of energy your home uses (look at the kWh usage on the bill)
- The average amount of peak sunlight in your area
  - West (as in California) about 6 ½ hours
  - South (as in Texas) about 5 ½ hours
  - Midwest (as in Nebraska) about 4 ½ hours
  - Northeast (like New Jersey) aout 4 hours
- The wattage of the panel that you purchase

Generally, you can expect to spend about $20-$60K on solar panels, even if it is 8 of them. But, there is an option for panels that is relatively new and may have me looking at solar savings on my roof again.

Solar Shingles Is A Thing?

Photovault (solar) shingles are indeed a thing. What's more is they appear and function like the traditional materials listed above such as asphalt and slate with the bonus of generating electricity.

The Department of Energy has cosigned on these bad boys saying that solar shingles can boost the value of your home--by over $15,000. They can perform this task for easily two to three decades. After that, solar shingles can still perform, but depreciate in their energy capacity.

Solar shingles are much smaller than solar panels, so they are more maneuverable. The peaks and valleys of your roof won't be such a large obstacle. As in, I could do my entire roof in solar shingles vs. 8 solar panels. Solar shingles are about 12" x 86" and weigh 13 lbs per foot.

The number of solar shingles it would take to power your home still depends on the above quantum physics (math, I just hate it), but size is not nearly as restrictive. Solar shingles are made of TFSC (thin-film solar cells of copper idiom gallium selenide). The energy conversion rate is at about 12%. Some PV single brands use monocrystalline silicon which are more expensive but boost efficiency rate (energy conversion) up to 20%.

Solar shingles have advantages and disadvantages that should be weighed and measured if you are considering 'going solar'. The manufacturer of the panels matters too in service, design, and warranty.

Pros	*Cons*
Aesthetically pleasing and sleek looking.	Not widely offered by companies and roof installers as of yet
If you are building a new home or replacing your roof, solar shingles are more cost-effective.	Not all solar shingles can be installed on an existing roof.
Can be removed and reinstalled elsewhere if you move.	If you decide on Tesla shingles with advanced options, you probably will need to build a new roof and there is a longer installation time

Depending on the brand, there is a vast difference in price and options. Pricing is composed of total square footage, energy needs, and manufacturer/installer. For standard solar shingles you are looking at between $15,000 to $20,000. Tesla has a highly specialized platform that can cost $70,000 plus.

What Is So Freaking Special About Tesla?

In late 2016, CEO Elon Musk announced his new solar shingles were coming and in April of 2018, Tesla, via their subsidiary SolarCity, rolled them out. Listening to feedback and improving upon the product, Tesla released the Solar Roof V3 in October of 2019. Musk backed the faith and durability in his product with a 25-year weatherization warranty.

Tesla's roof installations are a combination of *active* solar shingles and *non-active* solar shingles. Your entire roof is replaced with this combination. Solar cells are contained within the active solar tiles and produce the energy for your home use. Inactive shingles are *regular* shingles that do not produce energy. Tesla requires solar roofs to have the Tesla Powerwall which is a solar battery to store your home's energy. Tesla Powerwall is mandatory and the more of them you get, the less they cost.

As of June 2021, the Powerwall costs about $10,500 but there are incentives from Tesla and the government to deflect the cost. Which is why the price is no longer broken out and instead provided in the installation price. Demand for the Powerwall is high and production is struggling to keep pace, which is why installs with Tesla solar shingles have longer wait times and are not as convenient to deal with at present. The demand comes from being able to go completely off the power grid. Others may have shortages, like in Texas in 2021 - but you would not. So, the Powerwall is pretty sexy.

Tesla reports active solar tiles cost $2.01 per watt and the inactive tiles vary depending on your roof. They broke it down into three groups of roof for the cost of the inactive tiles:

- Simple = $14.00 per square foot
- Moderate = $16.00 per square foot; and
- Complex = $19.24 per square foot

There is no real way to figure out the cost of a Tesla solar roof other than a quote from Tesla. Tesla has required some consumers to upgrade their electrical panel to accommodate the shingles which was an up cost of roughly $5,000. So, it is best to contact them directly.

What makes Tesla roofs special? It is a roof *and* solar panels. Tesla's cost of $2.01 per watt is comparable to the US average of $2.85 per watt and you get more for your money. The thing is though, it may be more convenient and less costly - initially - to get solar panels than a whole new roof.

However, if you are building new or replacing your roof, it may be worth the cost vs the energy savings. Especially with all of the incentives, warranty, and federal tax credits.

Solar Reviews did a cost comparison an example - again, you would want to talk to Tesla about your specific roof, energy needs, etc:

	Tesla Solar Roof	Traditional solar install + roof replacement
Cost of solar after tax credit	$8,512	$12,021
Cost of roof replacement	$27,328	$8,540
Total Cost	$35,849	$20,561

Tesla provides a 25-year warranty on tiles, power, and weatherization. They also have a hail rating of up to 1.75" diameter and wind up to 166 mph. This makes them more durable than most solar panels. They also come with the highest fire rating. Another interesting fact is that their tiles are quartz based. This means optimum energy conversion.

If you decide Tesla may be the way to go, be prepared to upload your utility bills. They will also do a virtual assessment to see if your roof is a candidate. If it is, they go about getting the permits and doing the installation. Afterwards, the roof is inspected and approved. Then comes the coolness - you download the Tesla app to monitor the system's production and track the analytics. That is something that sets Tesla apart, well, along with the whole roof thing, oh, and the solar batteries.

If you are an avid Tesla fan, appreciate the technology, and love the roof aesthetics of your home then this is a swing and a hit. Tesla is leading in futuristic products for sustainability and continuously improving on products. Installing now may mean you are eligible for whatever they have in the works for future improvements.

If you are looking for something practical and less expensive that will get the job done - you may want to stick with the traditional means, especially if you enjoy customer service - Tesla is slacking in this department per recent reviews. But never fear, there are other companies in the race with Tesla on solar shingles.

Who Is Making A Name For Themselves In Solar Shingles?

Dow Chemical is in the running for a solid solar shingles product. RGS Energy believes in the product so much that they signed an exclusive agreement with Dow. RGS has been installing and servicing solar panels for over four decades and is servicing Dow's warranty agreements, so there is no lack of customer service or experience. The cost is between $3.89 to $4.74 per watt of solar power.

CertainTeed works a bit differently with solar shingles. Their solar shingles are installed as an integral element of the existing roof you have. This makes them the king of low profile solar roofs that are unobtrusive and work well with your existing roof. However, energy conversion ratings are at the lower end between 16 to 20%. The good news is, their average customer claims the installation covers 90-95% of their electricity bill.

Luma is the only brand offering an 'upgradable' solar roof shingle system. They have vast experience in the solar industry and are in over 20 states. Luma solar shingles boast a 21% conversion efficiency rate which is higher than solar panels. Their patented shingles allow for airflow and are smaller in size which means an earlier turn on time to start sucking the sun.

The benefits of incorporating a solar roof into your lifestyle can't be overstated. There are several choices, it is just a matter of picking the right one out for your lifestyle and energy needs. Although harnessing the sun's energy is a very old idea, it is just starting to come into acceptance and gaining traction in sleek design, efficiency, functionality, and price--for some anyway. The blossoming solar panel space reminds me of another space sitting beneath the roof that America took to another level, the front porch.

CHAPTER 18

Front Porches: An Origin Story

When I think of a grand front porch, my mind goes South. The movie *Gone With The Wind* features brilliant mansions and beautiful front porches. The movie was released in 1939 and the opening scene takes place on the eve of the Civil War. The story surrounds Scarlet's life.

Scarlet is a petulant Southern belle who survives the tumultuous era while simultaneously entangled in love affairs between Ashley Wilkes and Rhett Butler. The story is quite scandalous and one of my favorites. Everyone needs a Rhett Butler.

One of the homes in the movie, Twelve Oaks, was inspired by the home from the opening scene. It is an 1836 Greek Revival known as Whitehall which resides in Covington, Georgia. Greek Revival, huh? When it's not Romans or hippies it's apparently the Greeks.

Greek Revivals reflect classical architecture inspired by temples in ancient <u>Greece</u>; like the Parthenon. The luxurious style was dominant in the 1820s and through the Civil War era for private homes and public buildings; especially government buildings.

During this time period, America was exploring who she was and turned to Greece for architecture, philosophy, art, and ofcourse, democracy. Copying a culture is the highest form of flattery. Towns erupted with Greek names across America like: Athens, Ithaca, Sparta, etc.

Greek Revival architecture has common elements that set it apart and are easily recognized:

- Tall columns & pediments
- Painted plaster exterior (gives the pristine stone-look of Greek architecture)
- Horizontal transom
- Moldings (everywhere inside and out)
- Embellishment (second story attraction, pilasters, lots of pizzaz)

The grand entrances wrapped in porch pegs makes me think the Greeks invented front porches; however, that thought is under much debate. There are a few theories about who the trendsetters of front porches were.

A great many folk believe the origins of the front porch to be ancient and credit the usual suspects of ancient civilizations: Egyptians, Romans, and Greeks. However, there is one interesting story of origin that is not as prevalent as the others but makes a great deal of sense. The beginning of porches may have been in Africa.

Michael Dolan wrote *The American Porch - An Informal History of An Informal Place.* In the book, he surmised that during the 1400s (a bit after ancient civilization), European explorers were fascinated by the African dwellings and wrote about:

"dwellings (that) often featured an exterior space that functioned like a room; but was open on three-sides, and had a roof supported by poles. During the day, when the (dwelling's) interior became oven-like, these semi-public areas provided comparative comfort to conduct daily activities."

Climate plays a vital role in what kind of porch you have. Americans took the porch idea, whether it is from Greece or Africa, and ran with it. No other country has doted on this structure more, making it truly an *American* architecture.

Some people believe the roots of American porch infatuation are a result of colonial <u>trading</u> partners. Trading routes brought culture to our shore from everywhere and provided some influence. Traders hailed from the Caribbean, Britain, France, and Spain. The trader architecture influence meshed well with our diverse population.

Americans elevated the porch beyond its original purpose and designed it to connect home, and its occupants, to community and neighborhood in seamless fashion. Porches are seen as an extended handshake to the world; an invitation. It is where trust is established before entering the home and our beloved stoop to dish neighborhood dirt. Before the internet, we had our porchly perches to oversee the neighborhood.

In fact, trust not only flowed inward, it flowed outward. Trust was won with the American people from porches. In 1880, James Garfield successfully campaigned and won the presidential election from his porch. The political art was called *porch stumping* and was used well into the 1900s. Later, World War I and II limited resources to maintain and build grandiose porches and they became entirely extinct during the Great Depression.

The 1950s and 60s didn't appreciate lovely front porches either as suburban tract homes sprouted in fast-pace accompanied by those awesome set-back legislations. Quality seemed to give way to quantity. This adopted architectural strategy allowed for streamlined, less expensive and time-consuming builds. People were pushed to a large, private backyard for enjoyment. Modest homes for Americans lined the pockets of builders nicely. Then something happened.

In the 1970s (there are our hippies), historic preservation efforts and community movements prevailed. The new school of thought was a desire to live in older homes. Older homes had front porches. It was the revival period of grandiose front porches, hurray! Porches were drawn into new builds and residential construction. At the time, there was a strong need to connect with the community due to the previous years of hardship and competition for resources.

Today setbacks limit the acreage we can use for front porches, but most homes are equipped with basic features of a front porch. During the pandemic, front <u>porches</u> are a place we escape to for a piece of the outdoors and to shake cabin fever.

If you are fortunate enough to have the clearance for a front porch and want to add one, it will hit the pocket book to the tune of abot $21,000 on the average (300 square feet). The good news is that porches add value to the home and you will recoup about 90% of your renovation costs.

For people that use their front porch as storage, STOP IT! People will think you have no home training. American porches are our legacy and social lubricant - don't dirty that up.

CHAPTER 19

Smart Technology: Love It Or Hate It

If you are like me, you have a love/hate relationship with technology. Smart technology has grown by leaps and bounds. There are several ways that smart technology has saturated home development and design. The Internet of Things (IoT) has literally both scared and slightly aroused me. IoT is the ability for all of your technology to talk to each other *without* human intervention.

Internet Of Things (IoT)

Sounds like the start of a good horror Sci-Fi flick, right? Or, you could say IoT rallies devices under your complete control to be the master of your destiny and wield great power. IoT acts as your personal assistant controlling:

- Clocks
- Computers
- Smartphones
- Cameras
- Speakers
- Lights
- Doorbells

- Water Heaters
- Appliances
- Cooking utensils
- Pet Feeders
- Window Shades
- And more

If your house has a nervous system, IoT would be the hypothalamus. Simply put, everything in (and several things out) of your house links up to IoT. IoT is linked to your phone, Alexa, Google Nest, Ring, or whatever you are using to communicate and control your devices and appliances.

For example, if you say, *"Alexa, start the coffee,"* Alexa would start the coffee with a pleasant little *"Yes, Mistress,"* or whatever you designed her to say. If you are on vacation in Jamaica and your friend forgot the code to your door, you could pick up your smartphone and unlock the door to let him in *and* watch him feed the dog. Do you get the double-edged good and evil value of this?

If I were a teenager, I would absolutely loathe this technology because the days of autonomy and sneaking out are over. As a parent of two tweens and a 20+ year old that somehow can't do laundry at his house and whose version of going shopping is rifling through my pantry - I absolutely love this technology. So, it's all about perspective. She who wields the controls has the power. That last sentence may be why I am never allowed to touch the TV remote.

What should be noted is these devices do not need your input to talk to each other. Let's say your sprinkler system has a water leak underground that you can't see. The water meter will speak with the sprinkler system and report back to you (and/or your landscaper) through IoT. The system will identify that there is a leak, where it is, and repair or shut the sprinkler system off.

IoT can schedule the appointment with your landscaper without you having to insert yourself in the conversation. IoT is set to save you hundreds of dollars in water restriction fines and repairs by alerting the landscaper to where the leak is and what exactly is wrong. This AI saves you massive time as well as money. You can stay on the beach in Jamaica, no intervention needed.

The demand for IoT friendly devices has increased, and by 2021, you can expect there to be about 20 <u>billion</u> IoT smart devices with a 5G network. The average is about 13 connected devices per person in North America, with Europe trailing at an average of 9 devices per person. We as individuals have a harem of devices.

Does IoT have it's disadvantages, sure. Combined with AI, IoT could effectively take over our lives. In the movie iRobot with Will Smith, robots did take over because humans were incapable of acting in their own best interests. That theory is fairly spot on. I am my worst enemy.

It is incredibly likely that IoT will learn so much about your buying habits, right down to what you spent for facials, that it could do your taxes for you, ouch. Another likely disadvantage is that your life could be hacked into and held for ransom. This happens. Alot. Job security, definitely another issue as machines take over tasks.

There are a plethora of devices for the home that are mind boggling. For example, meal cookers that alert you when meat is cooked to perfection and robotic vacuum cleaners that sweep your floors within scheduled hours. There are too many to name. The devices that pertain to actual home design are what we will address here, not smart appliances that can be added by the homeowner at any time. Still, I will miss some.

Home Designers & IoT

The trick with IoT is that it usually leads to several different apps on your phone to control your devices. We need a home integration app to act as ONE hub for all IoT smart home devices. There are some out there that are <u>starting</u> to grasp the concept of this need, such as:

- SmartThings
- HomeKit
- Echo

But none have become a universal solution for all applications. Enter <u>Josh</u>. Josh is IoT married with artificial intelligence (AI). Josh can memorize daily commands like lowering the blinds at night or making you coffee in the morning. Josh gives me significant lady wood. It is like having a personal assistant that does what you want before you have to ask.

Josh is designed to work as an interface for several different things and is voice commanded as if you are talking to an old friend. The designers of Josh see the need for one interface in a world of smart applications.

The Basics of What Should Be Included

How do devices like Josh play out for home designers? <u>Purdue</u> developed a plan to implement IoT with home development plans. According to Purdue, the goal is in energy efficiency and collecting data to run physical devices efficiently.

Future home building should be embedded with sensors, network connectivity, etc., for smart devices to gather intel and exchange data for IoT controlled devices to be used optimally. According to Purdue, the goal is to create a home with IoT features that control:

- Temperature
- Humidity
- Movement/Security
- Water
- Power

All of which to be controlled by a mobile device. They have included a provision that the device must work while the power is out in the home, so a battery back-up and internet hot spot would be part of the deal.

In future home development, these items are going to be the staples for every American Home to ensure energy efficiency and capitalize on current resources. The good news for the project at Purdue, they had a budget of $300 to purchase the components, and they used about half of that.

Of course, this was an undergraduate study, but it is significant because the future of innovative and relevant engineering, architecture, and home development is exerting itself through our educational system. We will see their genius as they enter the workforce.

IoT is here now, and college students will perfect the process, but they have a valid point of what to include in the design of every American home as a basic ground zero package.

Amazon's Smarthomes

Amazon is in the race for the perfect smart home and has sunk $6.7 <u>million</u> into the competition with their smart home with voice technology. Amazon teamed up with a prefab builder while simultaneously launching Alexa Guard.

The goal is to make everything in the house voice-activated from the microwave to the clock on the wall that will set the time ahead and back automatically in correlation with daylight savings time. Their new smart home is pictured here: <u>https://www.loveproperty.com/</u>

Plant Prefab and Amazon are vested in providing affordable smart home automation to the masses ranging from $160,000 for a 400 sq. foot one-bedroom home to a 3100 sq. foot 5-bedroom home to the tune of a little over a million dollars. So, the 'affordable' may need a bit of tweaking.

What Other Home Builders Are Doing

Home Builders are taking different approaches to home building and who their customer is. Right now, it is the soccer mom, according to Meritage's M.Connected <u>home</u>.

"I think that's who you really want to focus on," Herro says. "It's not about starting with the technology. It's about catering to that 36-year-old mom, and figuring out what inspires her, what she will truly use, and what will make her life better."

The services that are coming standard in their Home Automation Suite are:

- Ring video doorbells
- Kwikset Kevo door locks
- iDevice & Leviton smart lighting
- Rachio, Hunter, Rainbird & Toro irrigation systems
- LiftMaster garage door openers
- Aprilaire thermostats
- Amazon's Alexa and Echo speakers

With an educational session on how to run the home. This is the arsenal of today's soccer mom. Lennar builders also implemented smart home technology as a standard with Everything's Included Wi-Fi certified homes. Their standard package includes:

- Amazon Echo Show and Dot
- Ring video doorbell
- Honeywell Thermostat
- Kwikset & Baldwin smart locks
- Lutron lighting
- Sonos music
- Samsung SmartThings hub

And a complimentary free session on how to run it all with 90 days of free support. Other builders are following suit, including:

- Pulte
- Centex
- Del Webb
- DiVosta

- John Wieland Homes and Neighborhoods
- KB Home
- TRI Pointe Group

Are partnering with Google or Amazon or both to deliver on the high-demand for smart home integrations. The IoT is coming correct with home builders, and the wave of Wi-Fi will be seen in new developments and communities more and more. With the increase in smart homes and their practical approach to soccer moms, you know that smart appliances will be upping their game to join in the revolution.

Love it or hate it, best make your peace with it.

CHAPTER 20

The Business End of It - You're Welcome

The Titanic was crafted with bold statements of being invincible with lush extravagance that would make royalty blush. The fact that it could sink, much less that it did so on its maiden voyage was unthinkable at the time.

In the 1980s, the Soviet Union was strong, formidable, and prosperous. No one could have imagined the drastic changes that led to the end of the cold war and redrawing of territories on maps.

Fukushima nuclear plant was a fortress of high sea walls filled with workers well-versed in emergency planning with extensive experience. They were ready for any situation. That is until a <u>tsunami</u> struck in March of 2011 causing the partial meltdown of three reactors.

What do all these stories have in common? They are Black Swan <u>events</u>. Black swan events are unpredictable, well beyond anything one would expect to happen, and are coupled with severe consequences on humanity - usually damaging the economy -- and describe anything from credit to war.

Black swan events are rare, severe, and as a cruel joke - they seem obvious in hindsight. Black swans are significant historical events.The key words there are '*seem obvious*'. You are probably wondering what this has to do with anything, let me provide some insight before I move into the point of this chapter.

In 2007, a finance professor and former Wall Street trader Nicholas Taleb wrote a book about the idea of a black swan event and has become the authority on what constitutes a black swan. He wrote the theory one year before the 2008 financial crisis. He encouraged people to operate as if a black swan event is a possibility and advised diversifying portfolios may afford some protection. He also advised normal strategy and schools of thought cannot forecast a black swan and might even make one more vulnerable to them.

The 2008 housing market crisis is considered a black swan event. It was catastrophic and global with only a few predicting that it would happen. I will let you in on a little secret - nothing from the 2008 housing crash was fixed inside financial institutions. The banks were bailed out without creating a new policy or lending structure to prevent such a collapse in the future - we are due for the same kind of crises within the next two years, the housing market is swelling as I type this (remember this when I get to commercial property, soon - laying groundwork takes a moment).

Now, the big question of the last few years is *"Was COVID a black swan?"* The answer is a resounding NO. Poor planning or response does not a black swan make. This was Taleb's response to COVID being referred to as a black swan. Unfortunately, events like COVID aren't rare and therefore it does not fit the criteria. Historically, it has happened about every 100 years and is the top mass killers of people, albeit more frequently as of late. Pandemics are a matter of *when*, not *if*.

In 2018 there was a research study that indicated:

"The probability of a pandemic of a certain level occurring is one in 100, or 1% in any given year. So, just as with a flood, when calculated fof a 30-year period, there is a greater than one in 4 chance of a pandemic occurring."

There is no argument that COVID will have a significant impact on the economy and it is way too early to recognize every consequence that has yet to unfold in severity but it will also not produce the global mortality rate of the 1918 flu outbreak.

Experts did warn, for decades, that a global pandemic involving a highly infectious respiratory disease virus was *plausible*. The only question was when. Smaller outbreaks were a precursor - Asian flu, Ebola, nipah, SARS, MERS, and H1N1- all this occurred since the beginning of the 20th century. Now this next bit is important, Ryan A. Bourne, author of *Economics in One Virus* wrote:

"It suits both CEOs and politicians to believe this and convince us that it [a black swan event] is true. If nobody could have possibly foreseen the pandemic, then it absolves politicians and businesses from many of their failures in preparing or reacting to the eventuality."

What he is saying is that by calling it a black swan, big business is eligible to be bailed out by the government with taxpayer money - no explanation needed. This should sound familiar as we just discussed it a few paragraphs ago and it happened in the big bank bail out.

There are a lot of moving parts there and they all move dynamically in tandem for a perfect storm, now to my point. Lurking ominously in the eye of this storm -- when you combine this historical background knowledge with residential and commercial reality, you get...Resident Evil.

The Commercial Hive

Resident Evil is a SciFi movie and the story takes place underneath Raccoon City. The 'Hive' is like a large commercial building that houses a genetic research facility. Scientists, workers and their families live, work, and play in this vast network of businesses, apartments, shops and schools underground.

The entire thing is operated by the Umbrella Corporation. The Umbrella Corporation is the mastermind guiding the research and funding this and many other such projects. A toxin is developed (it is a research facility after all) that turns people into the living dead ravenous for human flesh. The hero, Alice, is an unwilling participant and altered by an experiment while fighting the good fight against the powerful Umbrella Corporation and killing zombies along the way to end their tyranny and save the world.

The focus on this story goes to large commercial buildings. A few things are happening here. COVID has driven employees out of the office and into their homes. Remote work has proven to be more cost-effective for some large corporations - at least in part. People will go back to work, but not filling the office buildings in the same way as they did pre-COVID. Companies don't need to keep the lights on and have streamlined processes to work efficiently. Alot of the corporate entities won't need the space that they used before and will save a mountain of money on leases.

What does this mean? It means these hollowed out commercial buildings will need to be repurposed and technology is all the rage - we have smart homes, why not smarter buildings? Commercial parks will be renovated to feature floors for offices, restaurants, virtual reality rooms as retreats, gyms, apartments, grocery stores, hydroponic gardens, schools, playgrounds - entire communities safely tucked inside the confines of one building - an above-ground Hive. It is the next natural progression and a good strategy for large corporations that own large buildings but only require half the staff to be physically present at their job.

Apple has announced employees will go back to work 3 days a week with the option to work from home 2-weeks out of the year. Have you seen the size of Apple Park - the headquarters for Apple? Something tells me they will start condensing this space or allow employees to work full-time remotely from home -- if they live there -- renovating part of the campus for living quarters for some employees?

You can get a tour on YouTube at https://youtu.be/WmmC86fQ6QA

Apple Park is a Hive waiting to happen. Amazon employs nearly 92,000 globally. Can you imagine the office space they must hold? They <u>announced</u> certain employees can work remotely 2 days a week as well.

Atlassian is headquartered in Australia and has other offices scattered globally, including the US. They have announced all of their employees will be working remotely -- permanently. That is a lot of office space. Dropbox, FaceBook, Hubspot, Lambda School, Lincoln Financial Group, and LogMeIn followed suit with 100% remote employees.

Some companies are developing a hybrid system like Apple and Amazon. Microsoft is going to 50% remote and Paypal is following that path. The physical working environment is shifting. I think the next housing crisis, and there will be one, will provide a sense of urgency for this office space to become an affordable alternative for those caught in the throes of the violent housing market.

Evolution points to fundamental, functioning utopia communities - Hives. We definitely have the Umbrella corporations - and black swan bailouts - to fund such an endeavor. Investors will see the potential of creating the 'Hive' to receive royalties from every business and home located within the concrete capsule of consumers that are completely dependent on the enclosed amenities. This is about the same time that we will come out wth Tour 3 - The Hive Edition. But right now, we will settle with bathroom requirements.

Employment As A Lifestyle Choice

Now that we know about Hives, it would be prudent to have some foresight and speak on the requirement of office showers so these can be put in the renovations at an early stage. Let's talk about company perks.

Employers are becoming increasingly more invested in the physical and mental health of their employees. I would love to think that this is 100% altruistic, but let's be real - employee wellness correlates with happy workers, high morale, increased productivity, less health costs, and weighted benefits in place of salary bumps. Offering sexy wellness packages has benefits for employees and employers.

In 2019, 84% of large employers <u>offered</u> workplace wellness that included support in losing weight, smoking cessation, and lifestyle and behavior coaching. That means 63 million covered employees work for firms offering health benefits *and* workplace wellness.

Employers are also performing health screenings and asking employees to disclose extensive personal health information. You may know it as a health risk assessment (HRA). In 2019, 72% of large firms provided either an HRA or biometric screening, or both. Now that we are in the tech age, employers and their health plans have collected information through wearable means - 42 million covered employees.

These aren't ordinary health plans, they are health-contingent wellness programs. What does that mean? It means employers are offering a wellness incentive program based on health risks. A health contingent wellness program requires employees to:

- Meet a health standard
- Meet an alternate standard in order to earn an incentive or avoid penalty

These plans were authorized by federal regulation in 2006 and reinforced by the Affordable Care Act. These employers (54% of them) will provide financial incentives. They have done the math and know that prevention is more cost-effective than treating. Incentives come in the form of a fixed cash payout, discounts to employee's health premium contribution, or merchandise.

Right now, workers can opt not to participate in the wellness program to protect their privacy; however, it is not unheard of for penalties to be assessed to non-participating employees. Here is an example courtesy of KFF.org (insurance):

Yale University Health Expectation Program (HEP)

In 2017, Yale University implemented a new employee wellness program for its unionized clerical, technical, food service, and maintenance staff and their spouses. Employees and spouses covered by Yale medical plans are automatically enrolled in HEP, and then must follow screening recommendations. Those diagnosed with or having risk factors for certain conditions (such as diabetes, hypertension, or hyperlipidemia) can also be required to participate in a health coaching program. Trestle Tree is the wellness vendor that administers the health coaching program in partnership with a second vendor, HealthMine, which receives all health data on workers covered by the program. In addition to data collected through screening, health insurance claims data, including pharmacy claims, for all health plan enrollees is regularly transferred to HealthMine, regardless of whether enrollees participate in HEP.

Members may opt out of participating in HEP if they pay a weekly fee of $25, or $1,300 for the entire year, which is deducted from their paycheck. The average annual salary for a Yale food service worker is reportedly less than $37,000. HEP participants who don't comply with the program are also subject to the $25 weekly fee. In one reported case, a campus cook and breast cancer survivor who had undergone bilateral mastectomy was nonetheless told she would be fined $25/week unless she had a mammogram.

In 2019, this employee and several others brought a class action suit against Yale University, arguing that it coerces employees and their spouses to turn over health information in violation of the ADA and GINA, federal laws that permit collection of personal health information by employers only through voluntary wellness programs.

In response, Yale points out this wellness program was agreed to by the union as part of its collectively bargained health benefits package. Under the agreement, the HEP took effect in 2017, when EEOC regulations permitting wellness financial incentives were still in effect. Yale also argues the wellness program financial incentive is modest and does not render the choice to participate as involuntary.

Federal law permits collection of health information from workers through voluntary workplace wellness programs. This is intriguing when you consider the possibility of a Hive existence where you live, work, and play. It's almost like employers will be able to cultivate an employee garden in which they pick the finest stock out of the gene pool to live in the Hive and work for the company. It's increasingly interesting that I think the first one to make this move will be Apple who has a long history of firsts in motivating consumers *and* employees. How Matrix-ish. They will also undoubtedly have a magnificent gym - which brings me to the point of this entire chapter - office showers.

Office Showers Are A Requirement

We have established that Las Vegas is a furnace. When I had an office, I would have loved an office shower because I had to go outside alot and I would have appreciated (and I am sure my clients would have appreciated) somewhere to freshen up. On another note, with employers taking an invasive interest in health it would only make sense to have a gym - and a gym requires a shower.

There is no doubt, employees who exercise are more productive and are less likely to burn out on the job. Encouraging workplace physical and mental fitness can be both meditative (yoga) and physically demanding (cardio). Showers just make sense in this workplace culture and lifestyle. This would also support healthy, sustainable life skills such as riding a bike to work or exercising rather than smoking during breaks.

Workplace shower facilities <u>encourage</u> employees to arrive early and catch a half hour workout, freshen up, and feel energized for work and have a productive mindset without offending those around them. Fitness is a daily routine and can serve as a hiring perk to secure talented employees and attract those that value health.

Medical facilities and manufacturing plants would benefit from commercial showers so their work is not brought home with them in a mixture of sweat and soiled clothes. In hospitals, or other time-demanding occupations where shifts can be 24 hours - showers can help restore, wake up, and refresh employees to improve accuracy and efficiency.

If companies are going to be delving into the most intimate private areas of my life, the least they could do is extend the courtesy of a place to clean them and be hygienically fit. I am, after all, a representation of their company.

CONCLUSION

Playing house is at the core of imaginative play. Reaching back in your memory, your idea of what a home was changed and evolved as you grew older. You imagined what was practical, what was possible, and envisioned what could be. Somewhere on the bridge from child to adult, our imaginations become smaller.

Imaginations are swallowed by obligation. We work hard to own a home and then something happens where it starts to own us and we go along to get along. Those that keep their imaginations in full bloom are called innovators. Innovators quest to solve problems and give us time in the form of convenience. Time is the one commodity we can never get back.

In our view, it is the responsibility of professionals, those with expertise in all areas of life, to enhance the quality of life from one generation to the next. We are doing a piss poor job in the home development space, but I BELIEVE (#tedlasso), we can do better. Even the smallest of changes will send a ripple through the kingdom.

We have conformed to the 'it's always been done this way'. This book was meant to illuminate the possibilities and liberate current and future homeowners from settling. The world revolves around supply and demand. Demand better.

In the beginning of this book, it was promised you would not find easy answers, just a few interesting bits of information for the sake of conversation. Hopefully, you gained one nugget of knowledge you didn't know before about how we have the unique opportunity to be the bloody Romans and inspire innovation.

Challenges such as ordinances can deter common sense builds and design models that are ideal in form and function. Ultimately, popular opinion is what fuels change. You have the power and knowledge, how you wield that wisdom is up to you.

References In Order By Chapter

Chapter 1

https://www.unilad.co.uk/featured/this-is-how-much-of-your-life-youve-spent-on-the-toilet/

https://en.wikipedia.org/wiki/Diseases_and_epidemics_of_the_19th_century

https://www.oldhouseonline.com/kitchens-and-baths-articles/1920s-40s-baths

https://www.sunset.com/

https://candysdirt.com/2018/08/02/from-facebook-who-can-we-blame-for-the-carpet-in-the-bathroom-trend/

https://www.reddit.com/r/AskReddit/comments/5vzhtk/people_of_reddit_with_carpet_in_their_bathrooms/

https://www.cdc.gov/mold/control_mold.htm

https://www.bobvila.com/articles/carpet-in-bathroom/

https://www.warmup.com/blog/pros-cons-of-radiant-floor-heating

https://www.warmlyyours.com/en-US/posts/How-Much-Does-Floor-Heating-Cost-2574

Chapter 2

https://nchh.org/resource-library/fact-sheet_carpets-and-healthy-homes.pdf

https://aokcarpetcleaning.com/10-facts-dirty-carpets/

https://www.hgtv.com/design/remodel/kitchen-remodel/vinyl-flooring-in-the-kitchen

https://www.homeadvisor.com/cost/flooring/install-vinyl-or-linoleum-flooring/

Chapter 3

https://www.signalsdefense.com/blog/is-there-really-such-thing-as-a-one-way-mirror/

https://blog.solarart.com/one-way-mirror-film-vs.-one-way-mirror-glass

https://winsglass.en.alibaba.com/product/60420171244-802297088/Professional one way mirror glass for interrogation room of police office court.html

https://mcgrory.com/glass/one-way-vision/

Chapter 4

https://thescrubba.com/blogs/news/how-people-used-to-wash-the-fascinating-history-of-laundry

https://www.thoughtco.com/history-of-washing-machines-1992666

https://realloghomes.com/node/1084

https://www.homeadvisor.com/cost/laundry-rooms/#closing-article

https://dreamhousestudios.net/

https://www.theatlantic.com/technology/archive/2017/02/the-hidden-history-of-the-laundry-chute/516963/

https://laundryjet.com/residential-products/laundry-jet-plus/

https://www.katahdincedarloghomes.com/blog/laundry-jet/

https://www.finehomebuilding.com/2019/10/10/add-a-laundry-chute

Chapter 5

https://blog.thirdlove.com/asking-for-a-friend-seriously-what-is-a-balconette-bra-or-is-it-a-balcony-bra/

https://www.elitebalustrade.com/blog/a-brief-history-of-the-juliet-balcony/?v=79cba1185463

https://www.washingtonpost.com/archive/realestate/2002/04/27/once-common-attic-vanishes-as-houses-and-rooms-get-bigger/df1531d7-e883-4fb8-8231-56c41a67b862/

https://www.squareoneinsurance.com/resource-centres/getting-to-know-your-home/house-attic

https://www.homeadvisor.com/cost/walls-and-ceilings/raise-a-ceiling/

Chapter 6

https://www.lasr.net/travel/city.php?Louis+E.+May+Historical+Museum&TravelTo=NE0109007&VA=Y&Attraction_ID=NE0109007a002

https://www.rancholoscerritos.org/status-style-culture-interpretation-1870s-parlor-1931-living-room/#_ftn1

https://www.musingaroundlv.com/post/the-interesting-bizarre-world-of-sex-toys-from-top-to-bottom

https://playing-devils-advocate.captivate.fm/episode/sex-open-marriage-wait-what

http://www.searsarchives.com/homes/1908-1914.htm

https://jwselevator.com/elevators

https://www.insider.com/are-bidets-are-healthier-than-toilet-paper-2019-8

https://www.businessinsider.com/bidets-better-than-using-just-toilet-paper-2019-9

https://www.acentech.com/blog/singing-in-the-bathroom-acoustics-in-time-of-quarantine/

https://www.homeadvisor.com/cost/walls-and-ceilings/soundproof-a-room/#room

Chapter 7

https://www.sciencemag.org/news/2014/09/ancient-campfires-led-rise-storytelling#:~:text=Sometime%20about%20400%2C000%20years%20ago%2C%20humans%20learned%20to%20fully%20control%20fire.

http://www.mythencyclopedia.com/Dr-Fi/Fire.html#:~:text=The%20bringers%20of%20fire%20are,and%20gave%20it%20to%20humans.&text=In%20many%20versions%20of%20the,or%20other%20animal%20does%20so.

https://www.sciencemag.org/content/329/5993/743.summary

https://www.curioushistory.com/evolution-from-fire-to-fireplace/

https://www.oldhouseonline.com/interiors-and-decor/history-of-the-fireplace/#:~:text=The%20fireplace%20is%20a%20sparkling%20focal%20point%20in%20 historic%20homes.&text=The%20fireplace%20was%20a%20necessity,the%20nucleus%20 of%20family%20gatherings

https://www.huffpost.com/entry/the-evolutionary-reason-w_n_6171508

https://www.heatilator.com/shopping-tools/blog/look-to-gas-fireplaces-for-home-heating-help

https://www.fixr.com/costs/gas-fireplace

https://www.mansionglobal.com/articles/philadelphia-s-110-room-lynnewood-hall-gets-1-million-price-cut-75322

https://househistree.com/houses/lynnewood-hall

https://www.inquirer.com/life/inside-lynnewood-hall-abandoned-mansion-youtube-titantic-20200909.html

https://www.loveproperty.com/gallerylist/92978/tour-arlington-the-mysterious-abandoned-mansion-in-natchez-mississippi

https://autopsyofarchitecture.com/antebellum-arlington/

https://www.lovemoney.com/gallerylist/71317/incredible-stories-behind-abandoned-american-stately-homes

Chapter 8

https://www.forbes.com/sites/joemicallef/2017/12/20/exploring-romes-hidden-underground-city/?sh=5a295d866038

https://www.ranker.com/list/murder-rooms/jacob-shelton

https://clickamericana.com/topics/home-garden/vintage-basement-decor-from-40s-50s-see-25-creative-remodels

https://onmilwaukee.com/articles/fallout-shelter-spelunking

https://www.history.com/news/cold-war-fallout-shelter-survival-rations-food

https://www.rivertowns.net/news/971644-fallout-shelters-were-rage-50s-and-60s

https://www.dailymail.co.uk/news/article-2414497/Most-luxurious-bunker--The-1970s-Cold-War-Era-Home-built-26-feet-underground.html

https://www.menards.com/main/basement-walk-up-project-by-chris/c-5239772154538043.htm

https://askinglot.com/how-much-does-it-cost-to-build-a-walkout-basement-foundation#:~:text=Daylight%20or%20Walkout%20Basement%20Cost,requires%20extra%20excavation%20and%20grading.

https://homeguide.com/costs/foundation-cost#:~:text=A%20typical%20walkout%20basement%20costs,requires%20extra%20excavation%20and%20grading.

https://www.homeadvisor.com/cost/doors-and-windows/exterior-door/#:~:text=Installing%20a%20walkout%20basement%20door%20runs%20from%20%242%2C500%20to%20%2410%2C000,wall%20cut%20the%20appropriate%20size.

https://getbiggies.com/product-category/window-well-scenes/

https://www.nytimes.com/2020/08/14/realestate/coronavirus-home-improvement.html

Chapter 9

https://www.bbc.com/news/world-europe-41977709

https://finewineconcierge.com/a-history-of-fine-wine-storage

https://www.heritagevine.com/journal/the-history-of-wine-cellars/

https://www.housebeautiful.com/uk/lifestyle/news/a3357/household-features-success-status-symbol/

https://www.realtor.com/advice/home-improvement/wine-cellars-luxury-homes/

https://www.danby.com/blog/7-reasons-you-need-a-wine-cellar-in-your-home/

https://www.homeadvisor.com/cost/additions-and-remodels/build-wine-cellar/

Chapter 10

https://freshlawncare.com/blog/survey-says-americans-love-yards-important-to-homes-resale-value/

https://herald-review.com/survey-front-yards-get-custom-treatment/article_73b4e2c7-fa6a-5c1c-a63d-600b68867a3d.html

http://sites.bu.edu/dome/2018/07/19/the-problems-with-euclidean-zoning/

http://www.todayifoundout.com/index.php/2014/03/grass-lawns-2/

https://blogs.scientificamerican.com/anthropology-in-practice/the-american-obsession-with-lawns/

https://blogs.scientificamerican.com/anthropology-in-practice/the-american-obsession-with-lawns/

https://americanhistory.si.edu/america-on-the-move/city-and-suburb

https://rabble.ca/babble/humanities-culture/suburban-mentality

https://www.npr.org/2019/07/02/738131948/after-6-year-battle-florida-couple-wins-the-right-to-plant-veggies-in-front-yard

https://abcnews.go.com/US/vegetable-garden-brings-criminal-charges-oak-park-michigan/story?id=14047214

http://sites.bu.edu/dome/2018/07/19/the-problems-with-euclidean-zoning/

https://www.chicagotribune.com/entertainment/ct-ent-lawns-20171002-story.html

https://www.gardenrant.com/2013/01/no-front-yard.html

https://tort.laws.com/nuisance/use-enjoyment-of-private-property/interference-w-use-enjoyment-of-private-property

https://www.crcog.net/vertical/sites/%7B6AD7E2DC-ECE4-41CD-B8E1-BAC6A6336348%7D/uploads/Zoning_Validity_Challenges_Handbook.pdf

https://www.planning.org/join/all/

Chapter 11

https://www.builddirect.com/blog/history-of-the-backyard-as-we-know-it-a-long-form-read/

https://jayfencing.com/top-20-super-privacy-fence-designs/

https://homeguide.com/costs/fencing-prices

https://snowbrains.com/brain-post-much-time-average-american-spend-outdoors/

https://www.homeadvisor.com/cost/outdoor-living/install-a-patio-or-pathway/#:~:text=Installing%20a%20patio%20costs%20anywhere,to%20%2415%20per%20square%20foot.

https://www.bbqguys.com/bbq-learning-center/outdoor-kitchens/planning/6-essentials-elements#:~:text=1%3A%20Start%20With%20The%20Basics,compact%20refrigerator%2C%20and%20trash%20bin.

https://williamsonsource.com/the-ultimate-pool-luxury-outdoor-kitchen-and-living-space/

https://brownjordanoutdoorkitchens.com/blog/benefits-of-an-outdoor-kitchen/

https://www.npr.org/sections/coronavirus-live-updates/2020/03/27/822514756/fearing-shortages-people-are-planting-more-vegetable-gardens

https://www.gardencentermag.com/article/national-gardening-survey-2016/

https://squarefootgardening.org/

https://www.prnewswire.com/news-releases/26-of-us-consumers-planted-food-gardens-because-of-coronavirus-reports-packaged-facts-301222349.html

https://www.gardencentermag.com/article/scotts-miracle-gro-shares-gardening-statistics-covid-19/

https://www.nwf.org/Home/Latest-News/Press-Releases/2020/05-05-20-2020-National-Gardening-Survey

https://www.irmi.com/articles/expert-commentary/underground-construction-risks

https://www.homebiogas.com/product/bio-toilet-kit/

https://www.outdoorhappens.com/best-off-grid-toilet-options/

https://incinolet.com/

https://www.barnstablecountyhealth.org/resources/publications/compendium-of-information-on-alternative-onsite-septic-system-technology/incinerating-toilets

https://books.google.com/books?id=U3rJxPYT32MC&pg=PA478&lpg=PA478&dq=

The+Guide+to+United+States+Popular+Culture+fred+schroeder+lawn+ornaments&source=bl&ots=orbff7zEFS&sig=0MSfvOYVmL5TeKAtgRlxYqSk0jU&hl=en&sa=X&ved=2ahUKEwitjOTnxuPeAhWjxVkKHQBXBuQQ

http://lindaksienkiewicz.com/another-goose-in-clothes-spotted/#:~:text=

The%20lawn%20goose%20first%20appeared,the%20ornamental%20lawn%20goose%20family.

Chapter 12

https://www.britannica.com/topic/urban-planning

https://slate.com/news-and-politics/2013/07/photographer-george-steinmetz-arrest-how-much-airspace-do-you-own.html

https://www.triplecrowncorp.com/strange-housing-laws/

https://adata.org/faq/does-ada-cover-private-apartments-and-private-homes

https://www.ada.gov/regs2010/titleIII_2010/titleIII_2010_regulations.htm#a207

Chapter 13

https://www.homeadvisor.com/cost/environmental-safety/hire-an-insect-control-service/

https://natran.com/how-to-make-sure-your-home-is-sealed-from-pests-and-other-rodents-during-the-winter-months/

https://sfenvironment.org/sites/default/files/fliers/files/final_ppbd_guidelines_12-5-12.pdf

Chapter 14

https://www.garageliving.com/blog/garage-history-2/

http://www.blueskybuilders.com/blog/history-american-garages/

https://www.garageliving.com/blog/home-garage-stats/

https://home.howstuffworks.com/home-improvement/heating-and-cooling/improve-energy-efficiency-garage.htm

https://www.garageliving.com/products/garage-flooring/

Chapter 15

https://www.gazebo.com/blog/5-garden-gazebo-benefits/

https://www.thespruce.com/what-is-a-gazebo-used-for-2736944

https://www.fifthroom.com/gazebos/?gclid=CjoKCQjwk4yGBhDQARIsACGfAeuCca2u6EXF NZppULQRUZAtRDXGjrmAGTG7vLkLuc7JUiameQ-7OrsaAgNWEALw_wcB

https://www.bestinbackyards.com/photo-gallery?gallery=pool-houses

https://www.creia.org/the-development-of-our-building-codes#:~:text=Actually%20they%20can%20be%20traced,specified%20materials%20for%20roof%20coverings.

https://literarydevices.net/an-englishmans-home-is-his-castle/

Chapter 16

https://www.progressivefoam.com/will-vinyl-siding-increase-my-homes-value/

https://www.ebyexteriors.com/blog/siding/benefits-of-new-siding

Chapter 17

https://www.usatoday.com/story/news/nation/2019/12/11/pigeons-wearing-cowboy-hats-las-vegas-prompt-bird-rescue-operation/4396105002/

https://no1homeroofing.com/five-common-types-of-residential-roofing/

https://www.harryhelmet.com/the-best-roofing-materials-for-your-geographic-area/

https://www.solarreviews.com/blog/how-many-solar-panels-do-i-need-to-run-my-house

https://www.energysage.com/solar/calculator/

https://www.solarreviews.com/blog/tesla-solar-roof-do-the-solar-shingles-match-the-hype

Chapter 18

https://www.hgtv.com/design/decorating/design-101/greek-revival-architecture

https://napacountylandmarks.org/the-heritage-and-history-of-the-american-porch/

https://www.oldhouseonline.com/gardens-and-exteriors/history-of-old-house-porches/

https://www.lisafinks.com/front-porches-popular-again/

https://www.lisafinks.com/front-porches-popular-again/

Chapter 19

https://www.softwaretestinghelp.com/iot-devices/

https://www.toptal.com/designers/interactive/smart-home-domestic-internet-of-things

https://www.josh.ai

https://www.smartthings.com

https://www.apple.com/uk/shop/accessories/all-accessories/homekit

https://www.pfw.edu/departments/etcs/depts/ece/senior-design/iot-smart-house.pdf

https://www.loveproperty.com/news/77735/
amazon-build-prefab-smart-homes-with-integrated-alexa-to-beat-google

https://www.loveproperty.com/

https://www.builderonline.com/design/technology/for-many-builders-smart-homes-now-come-standard_o

Chapter 20

https://curiousmatic.com/top-black-swan-events-recent-history/

https://www.investopedia.com/terms/b/blackswan.asp

https://www.newyorker.com/news/daily-comment/
the-pandemic-isnt-a-black-swan-but-a-portent-of-a-more-fragile-global-system

https://theconversation.com/coronavirus-is-significant-but-is-it-a-true-black-swan-event-136675

https://dx.doi.org/10.2471%2FBLT.17.199588

https://www.rgare.com/knowledge-center/media/covid-19/
covid-19-brief-is-the-novel-coronavirus-pandemic-a-black-swan-considerations-for-insurers

https://www.livemint.com/opinion/online-views/covid19-pandemic-is-not-a-black-swan-event-11621182126326.html

https://www.flexjobs.com/blog/post/companies-switching-remote-work-long-term/

https://www.kff.org/private-insurance/issue-brief/
trends-in-workplace-wellness-programs-and-evolving-federal-standards/

http://cascadebusnews.com/shower-facilities-work-win-win-employers-employees/

Printed in the United States
by Baker & Taylor Publisher Services